Ranulph Higden

Ars componendi sermones

DALLAS MEDIEVAL TEXTS AND TRANSLATIONS

SPONSORED BY

UNIVERSITY OF DALLAS

DALLAS MEDIEVAL TEXTS AND TRANSLATIONS
2

Ranulph Hidgen
Ars componendi sermones

TRANSLATED
BY

Margaret Jennings (St. Joseph's College Brooklyn) and
Sally A. Wilson (Sacramento, Calif.)

INTRODUCTION AND NOTES
BY

Margaret Jennings

PEETERS
PARIS – LEUVEN – DUDLEY, MA
2003

Cover illustration: A monk preaching on Ps. 83.10 ("Better one day in your courts than a thousand elsewhere"). From a fifteenth-century French manuscript (MS. Valenciennes, *Bibliothèque municipale* 230, fol. 57). By kind permission of Bridgman Art Library.

Library of Congress Cataloging-in-Publication Data
Higden, Ranulf, d. 1364.
[Ars componendi sermones. English]
Ars componendi sermones / Ranulph Higden ; translated by Margaret Jennings and Sally A. Wilson ; Introduction and notes by Margaret Jennings.
p. cm. -- (Dallas medieval texts and translations ; 2)
Includes bibliographical references and index.
ISBN 9042912421 (alk. paper)
1. Preaching--Early works to 1800. I. Jennings, Margaret. II. Wilson, Sally A. III. Title. IV. Series

BV4209 .H5413 2003
251'.009'023--dc21 2002035794

ISBN 90-429-1242-1
D. 2003/0602/10

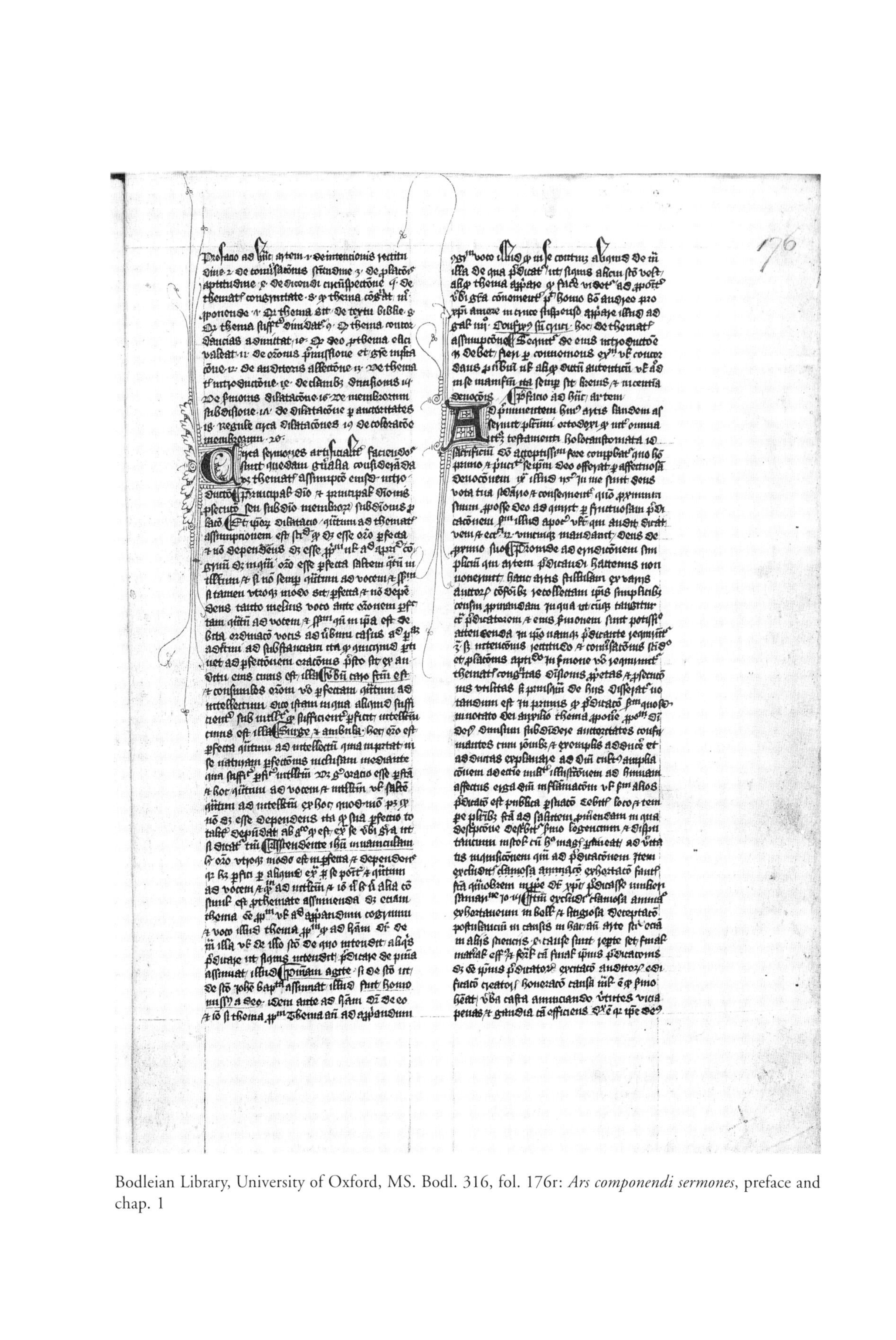

Bodleian Library, University of Oxford, MS. Bodl. 316, fol. 176r: *Ars componendi sermones*, preface and chap. 1

Editor's Foreword

The Dallas Medieval Texts and Translations series pursues an ambitious goal: to build a library of medieval Latin texts, with English translations, from the period roughly between 500 and 1500, that will represent the whole breadth and variety of medieval civilization. Thus, the series will be open to all subjects and genres, ranging from poetry through philosophy, theology, and rhetoric to treatises on natural science. It will include, as well, medieval Latin versions of Arabic and Hebrew works. In the future, the publication of vernacular texts is a possibility. Placing these texts side by side, rather than dividing them in terms of the boundaries of contemporary academic disciplines, will, we hope, contribute to a better understanding of the complex coherence and interrelatedness of the many facets of medieval written culture.

In consultation with our distinguished board of editorial advisers, we have established principles that will guide the progress of the series. The primary purpose of the Dallas Medieval Texts and Translations is to render medieval Latin texts accessible in authoritative modern English translations; at the same time the series will, however, strive to provide reliable texts in Latin where such are not yet available. The translations will therefore be established either on the basis of existing good critical editions (which we will not normally reprint) or, when necessary, on the basis of new editions. To enhance the accessibility of the texts to a large academic public, including graduate students, the critical apparatus of the editions will be limited to important variants. Each volume will comprise scholarly introductions, notes, and annotated bibliographies.

Works published in the Dallas Medieval Texts and Translations series will be unexcerpted and unabridged. In the case of a work too long to appear in a single volume, we will start with the beginning of the work or publish integral parts of it, rather than creating a selection of discontinuous texts.

The second volume of the Dallas Medieval Texts and Translation presents the fruits of a collaborative project that was suggested to the editors by Professor James Murphy, one of the great pioneers of the study of medieval rhetoric. In 1991, Ranulph Higden's *Ars componendi sermones* appeared in the Davis Medieval Texts and Studies series (published by Brill); it was edited by Professor Margaret Jennings of St. Joseph's College, Brooklyn. That same year, Sally A. Wilson devoted her Master's thesis at the California State University, Sacramento, to translating this *Art of Composing Sermons.* For our series, Ms. Wilson has reviewed and updated her thesis. On the basis of this work, Professor Jennings has prepared the thoroughly revised translation printed in this volume. Professor Jennings has also written an introduction which explains the genesis of the *artes praedicandi* and situates Ranulph Higden's concise and usable text (composed around 1346) among the more classically-oriented members of the genre. The rise of these manuals of preaching in the early thirteenth century and their subsequent development parallel what Jennings calls "the transformation of the ancient homily into the thematically developed medieval sermon." While her introduction elucidates the factors that led to this momentous change, her notes shed light upon details in Ranulph Higden's text which could present difficulties for the contemporary reader.

Thanks are due, in the first place, to the University of Dallas, whose financial support has made this series possible. Professor Glen Thurow, formerly Provost and Dean of Constantin College, believed in this project years before the first contributor submitted a manuscript. His successor, Professor Thomas Lindsay, has continued the University's generous assistance. Emmanuel and Paul Peeters enthusiastically embraced the idea for the Dallas Medieval Texts and Translations when we first discussed it with them in 1998. We are very pleased that our new series is associated with a publisher of such great tradition and renown. Thanks are also due to the medievalists in the United States and abroad who have agreed to serve on our board of editorial advisers.

Philipp W. Rosemann
July, 2002

Table of Contents

Introduction

The *Ars componendi sermones* of Ranulph Higden gives vibrant medieval life to the trite "last but not least." Written by this Benedictine monk of St. Werbergh's Abbey (Chester)[1] about 1346, the text is chronologically last among the arts of preaching whose organization conforms to the patterns established in Ciceronian *dispositio*. Yet its position is decidedly fortunate since Ranulph was able to incorporate the clarifications in theory developed by his predecessors as well as avoid the structural infelicities which characterized earlier treatises. Consequently, his *Ars componendi sermones* is arguably the most practical and user-friendly of the many *artes praedicandi* which were composed between 1220 and 1350.

I.

As a genre of medieval rhetoric — and sister to the arts of letter writing *(dictamen)* and of poetry — the *artes praedicandi* arose from the convergence of several phenomena in the later twelfth century. The most easily demonstrable is that era's interest in Ciceronian rhetoric. As the numerous surviving texts and glosses show, this period can be called the "apogee of the rhetorical movement in the Middle Ages."[2] But from the array of Cicero's important works, schools emphasized his early *De inventione* and the anonymous *Rhetorica ad Herennium* which was attributed to him.[3] The effect of this concentration was a highlighting of the process of *dispositio* or arrangement with its elements of inspiration, narration, division, confirmation, refutation, and peroration.

[1] For a brief survey of Higden's monastic experience, see Margaret Jennings, "Higden's Minor Writings and the Fourteenth Century Church," *Proceedings of the Leeds Philosophical and Literary Society* 16 (1977), 149–58, at 149–51; more detailed information can be accessed in notes 9, 10, 11, 15, 17, and 23 of this article.

[2] John O. Ward, "From Antiquity to the Renaissance: Glosses and Commentaries on Cicero's *Rhetorica*," in *Medieval Eloquence*, ed. James J. Murphy (Berkeley: University of California Press, 1978), 25–67, at 45.

[3] All citations to these classical works will be taken from *Ad C. Herennium*, trans. Harry Caplan, Loeb Classical Library (Cambridge, MA: Harvard University Press, 1954) and Marcus Tullius Cicero, *De Inventione*, trans. H. M. Hubbell, Loeb Classical Library (Cambridge, MA: Harvard University Press, 1949).

In the section on inspiration or *exordium*, the youthful Cicero concentrated on preparing a listener's mind for the rest of the speech. The elements involved in making an auditor well-disposed, receptive, and attentive — that is to say, striking material, concise and incisive development, and sincerity in presentation — are clearly described in *De inventione*, 1.16.23 and 1.15.20. In sum, the *exordium* should be sententious and serious and contain everything which will commend the speaker to his audience (1.18.25).

The second part of an oration, the *narratio*, explains incidents which have occurred or are supposed to have occurred. Among the several kinds of narration, Cicero's second, in which a digression is made for purposes of vituperation, comparison, amusement, or amplification, is especially noteworthy as is his recognition of its varied properties: "fabulous," "historical," "argumentative" (1.19.27–1.20.28). Brevity, clarity, and plausibility are again emphasized.

Clarity is also the object of a correctly made partition (*partitio*), which may take two forms: the first explains areas agreed and disputed; the second methodically sets forth matters to be discussed (1.22.31), allowing the auditor to focus on the salient points in the controversy. This type of *partitio* should also be brief, clear, and pointed, qualities which are thoroughly explained. Finally, the orator is counselled to complete the partition's sections in the same order in which they have been set forth (1.23.33).

Cicero then proceeds to define *confirmatio* as that part of an oration which, by marshalling arguments, lends credit, authority, and support to a particular cause; he stresses that it is the embellishment of an argument once it has been developed and the arrangement of it in definite divisions which make the speech attractive to an audience (1.30.50). This double and "much neglected" process is placed under confirmation so that the subject of "invention of arguments" may be combined with the theory of argumentation. Modes of argumentation — induction and deduction — are subsequently defined and illustrated, with the latter receiving very lengthy treatment. Its instrument, the syllogism, is also discussed (1.25.60) and the section concludes with an appeal for diversity in the elaboration of a *confirmatio* because "monotony is the mother of boredom" (1.41.76).

Obviously, Cicero's explanations of *refutatio* and *peroratio* have minimal reference to thematic sermon construction. More relevant to the twelfth century's understanding of *dispositio* is the *Rhetorica ad Herennium*'s contention that arrangement can be twofold: that which arises from rhetorical principles and that which is accommodated to particular circumstances.[4] The most notable feature of the former occurs in the rules for argumentation which, says the Auctor, should follow the sequence of proposition,

[4] *Ad C. Herennium*, 3.9.16–18.

reason, proof of the reason, embellishment, and resume.[5] In the second type, a departure from the normal Ciceronian order is allowed if the cause itself obliges the orator "to modify with art the arrangement prescribed by the rules of the art" (3.10.17).

Intense study of the *De inventione* and the *Rhetorica ad Herennium* made for a rhetorical competence which, combined with the twelfth century's pygmies-on-shoulders-of-giants confidence and a widening literacy, inspired a growing number of newly composed writings. Some were intended to assist in oral delivery and others were oriented towards a book-reading or book-using public.[6] Among those in the latter category, the *artes dictaminis* were most readily related structurally to the parts of an oration. In fact, by 1135, the anonymous *Rationes dictandi* had already developed a quasi-Ciceronian, five-part letter form.[7] The *Rationes* suggested that all letters begin with a *salutatio* or formal greeting of the addressee by his titles and with a *captatio benevolentiae*, an introduction proper, in which good will was sought. Both sections are easily related to the operations of the *exordium*. Certainly, an honorific and laudatory greeting is in line with its primary function: to bring the mind of the listener into a proper condition to receive the rest of the speech. The *captatio benevolentiae* resembles that species of the *exordium*, the *principium*, which has for its object the perfecting of good will, docility, and attention in the audience. The letter-writing treatises go on to make *narratio* the very next section in direct agreement with Ciceronian disposition. *Partitio* is, in general, omitted, although there may be some definite separation of parts in both the *narratio* and the *petitio*, the latter allowing for a presentation of requests along with arguments favoring their fulfillment. The argumentative portion of the *petitio* resembles Ciceronian *confirmatio*, which advocates the use of many different types of persuasion in proving the speaker's case. As might be surmised, the *ars dictaminis* omits the *refutatio* and modulates the *peroratio* or final summation into a simple *conclusio*.

The letter divisions defined in the *Rationes dictandi* passed into the manuals of several Bolognese masters and were a vibrant part of rhetorical doctrine throughout the twelfth century. They are found in the *Summa dictaminum* of Bernard of Bologna (1143–53), the *Summa Bernardina*, the *Ars dictandi Aurelianensis*, and the *Floribus rhetoricis* (all early 1180s), and the *Libellus de arte dictandi rhetorice*

[5] Ibid., 1.18.27.

[6] Michael Clanchy, *From Memory to Written Record* (Cambridge, Eng.: E. Arnold, 1979), 84.

[7] Charles Homer Haskins, *Studies in Medieval Culture* (New York: F. Ungar, 1958), 181. A useful history of the *artes dictaminis* is available in James J. Murphy, *Rhetoric in the Middle Ages* (Berkeley: University of California Press, 1974), 194–268; see especially p. 220 and pp. 222–8. Martin Camargo has intensively studied the genre in *Ars dictaminis, ars dictandi* (Turnhout: Brepols, 1991) and provided texts in *Medieval Rhetorics of Prose Composition* (Binghamton, NY: Medieval and Renaissance Texts and Studies, 1995).

(ca. 1185).[8] The *Libellus* is particularly important because its English provenance extends westward the previously pervasive Italian and French influence in the composition and dissemination of the letter-writing treatises.

Although the prescriptive tradition in the *artes dictaminis* was supplanted by the illustrative one in the thirteenth century, Ciceronian structures remained sufficiently ascendant among those interested in preaching to insure that manuals which were analogous to, though not dependent upon, their classical forebears would be composed. Such is clearly the case in the extensive thematic sermon textbook written, about 1220, by Thomas Chobham, well known English author of the *Summa Confessorum*. Called the *Summa de arte praedicandi*,[9] Chobham's treatise is the first large-scale effort to adapt classical rhetorical concepts to a medieval preaching context. Its rhetorical doctrine is much more complete than that of the nearly contemporary and exceedingly brief *De artificioso modo predicandi* of Alexander of Ashby, which avers that, although classical rhetoric can aid the preacher, it is less significant than an intangible "grace of speaking."[10] By contrast, the *Summa*'s first six sections analyze in detail the nature and species of preaching, recommend that the sermon condemn vice and extol the theological and cardinal virtues, and stress the importance of the speaker's reputation and character. In part 7, labeled "de arte praedicandi," Chobham explains the parts of an oration and then the parts of the art of rhetoric but, despite claiming familiarity with the *De inventione* and *Rhetorica ad Herennium*, he does not tie the former to *dispositio*. Chobham also seems uncertain about the relationship between *dispositio* and sermon structure; perhaps because of this and because of his lengthy investigation of *inventio*, he collates the first and second of rhetoric's parts as the following seriatim chapter list indicates: "De inventione"; "De inventione in exordio"; "De inventione in narratio"; "De inventione in divisionibus"; "De inventione in confirmatione et confutatione."

---

[8] See Haskins, *Studies*, 182–7 and Martin Camargo, "The *Libellus de arte dictandi rhetorice* Attributed to Peter of Blois," *Speculum* 59 (1984), 16–41. Camargo translates the salient points in the latter text in the first section of his *Medieval Rhetorics*.

[9] See Thomas Chobham, *Summa de Arte Praedicandi*, ed. Franco Morenzoni, CCCM 82 (Turnhout: Brepols, 1988). Chobham had certainly internalized the *Ad Herennium*'s (1.2.3) definition of *ars*: "Ars est praeceptio quae dat certam viam rationemque dicendi." Chobham's *Sermones* have also been edited by Morenzoni (Turnhout: Brepols, 1991); both texts have been extensively analyzed by him in *Des écoles aux paroisses: Thomas Chobham et la promotion de la prédication au début du XIIIe siècle* (Paris: Études Augustiniennes, 1995).

[10] Franco Morenzoni, "Aux origines des *Artes praedicandi*: *De artificioso modo predicandi* d'Alexandre d'Ashby," *Studii Medievali*, 3rd series, 32 (1991), 907–18, at 908. Franco Morenzoni also discusses Alexander in "Parole du prédicateur et inspiration divine d'après les *Artes praedicandi*," in *La parole du prédicateur, V–XVe siècles*, ed. Rosa Maria Dessi and Michel Lauwers, Collection du Centre d'études médiévales de Nice 1 (Nice: Centre d'études médiévales, 1997), 271–90, at 275–6.

Recognizing that *confutatio* is an almost impossible component of preaching, he quickly proceeds to a discussion of *memoria* and then to *dispositio*, which receives unusual and minimal treatment in terms of classical rhetoric since it functions, says Chobham, as a kind of organizing principle whereby reason and authority can be joined so as to create persuasive sermons.[11]

II.

In fairness, one should not expect a pioneering text like Chobham's to reflect the mature engagement with sources that is demonstrated in later and fully developed *artes praedicandi*. Consequently, some imperfect understandings of terms and their significance,[12] comparable to those noted in his discussion of *dispositio*, characterize Chobham's treatment of material related to the second element to affect the rise of the *artes praedicandi* — the metamorphosis of grammar. Grammar's change from a classical linguistic to a medieval speculative science is universally attributed to the revival of Aristotelian logic, a phenomenon which was to affect the trivium immensely and leave a mark on both education and scholarship.[13] The change was, of course, not sudden; a predilection to reason about facts instead of just observing them is demonstrable even in Carolingian authors.[14] In the eleventh century William of Conches had specifically proposed that logical structures be permitted to infiltrate grammatical investigation. In fact, the practice of employing the procedures of dialectic within the several arts of discourse is usually traced to his criticism of earlier grammarians for failing to discuss the *cause inventionis*.[15] *The Summa* of Petrus Helias follows the advanced program outlined by William, systematizes these *cause*, and underscores the preoccupation of twelfth-century glossators on Priscian with questions of logic.[16] Their equally deep

[11] "… in predicatione, quedam partes predicationis habent efficaciam ex ipsa virtute auctoritatis que inducitur, que per se sufficit ad probationem; alie autem partes predicationis virtutem habent persuadendi ex eo quod una auctoritas vel una ratio coniungitur cum alia, quarum utraque esset infirma per se, coniuncte tamen valent" (Chobham, *Summa*, 299).

[12] Chobham provides cursory treatment of divisions by substance and accidents and offers a jejune commentary on the significations of the *voces*; see *Summa*, 285.

[13] See G. L. Bursill-Hall, *Speculative Grammars of the Middle Ages* (The Hague: Mouton, 1972), 25–31.

[14] Charles M. Thurot, *Notices et extraits de divers manuscrits latins pour servir à l'histoire des doctrines grammaticales au moyen âge* (Paris: Imprimerie nationale, 1874), 117.

[15] Richard W. Hunt, "Studies on Priscian in the 11th and 12th Century," *Medieval and Renaissance Studies* 1 (1941), 194–231, at 212.

[16] Ibid., 214.

concern with questions of method and Petrus Helias' inability to downplay the dominance of dialectic practically insured its status as the Middle Ages' premier educational technique.[17] Ralph of Beauvais, Hugutio of Pisa, and Peter of Spain, involved as they were in the re-examination of the nature of language, found dialectic essential to their arguments.[18] Its methodology provided the scientific basis which the contemporary intellectual paradigm demanded and enabled grammar to express its theoretical interest in the truth and falsity of propositions, as well as its practical interest in the application of logical analysis to the meaning of words.[19] In the thirteenth century, this analysis would devolve into a refinement of many of the philosophical distinctions made by Petrus Helias and ultimately become the foundation for speculative grammar; its twelfth-century offshot seems to be the development of the verbal distinction, rooted in the Bible.

A biblical distinction operates in a twofold manner: it details possible figurative meanings for a certain word and then supplies text(s) in which the word is used to convey the meanings specified.[20] By nature schematic rather than discursive, the distinction explores a word's theoretical relationships, eschewing any attempt to explain an entire passage. Its origin and widespread acceptance in the later twelfth century is doubtless closely linked to the emergence of the thematic sermon.[21] As preachers focused on selected verses rather than pericopes, they insured the usefulness and occasioned the inevitability of the *distinctio*.[22] As a consequence, between approximately 1189 and 1200, five major collections of distinctions were produced, most oriented to the compositions of sermons.[23] Worth underscoring, however, is the fact that the emphasis on a word's significations and the preacher's subsequent usage of this tool developed out of the metamorphosis of grammar. Grammar's evolved *raison d'être*, which included the application of logical analysis to the meaning of words and the espousal of the dialectical method, provided the intellectual impetus for the dissecting of scriptural texts by means of multiple argumentative processes, that is to say, a schema similar to that of the thematic sermon.

---

[17] Ibid., 220.

[18] Robert H. Robbins, *Ancient and Mediaeval Grammatical Theory in Europe* (London: Bell, 1951), 89.

[19] Richard W. Hunt, "Studies on Priscian in the Twelfth Century, II," in *The History of Grammar in the Middle Ages*, ed. G. L. Bursill-Hall (Amsterdam: Benjamins, 1980), 39–94, at 64.

[20] Richard Rouse and Mary Rouse, "*Statim invenire*: Schools, Preachers, and New Attitudes to the Page," in *Renaissance and Renewal in the Twelfth Century*, ed. Robert Benson and Giles Constable (Cambridge, MA: Harvard University Press, 1982), 201–25, at 213.

[21] Ibid., 217.

[22] Ibid., 218.

[23] Ibid., 213–4.

The development of the distinction was not the only result of the logicization of grammar. That art's twelfth-century concern with ways of speaking as well as with modes of being — of posing questions *in voce* as well as *in re* — coupled with the age's desire to apply dialectical methodology directly to the realm of religious concepts,[24] had other palpable effects on the rise of the thematic sermon manual. To explore a tenet *in voce* one engaged in disputation, the first component of which, in the twelfth century, was *positio*.[25] *Positio* imposed the obligation to grant all that followed from a statement and to deny all that was incompatible with it,[26] and such necessity typed the reception of the theme from the earliest treatises onward. The dialectical methodology espoused by grammar probably underlay the thematic sermon's analysis of a scriptural text through its several possible divisions. Further, dialectic's emphasis on syllogistic reasoning was reflected in most *artes praedicandi* as was its interest in grammaticality or *congruitas*.[27] Finally, concordance, which was an effort to make the *res* (the transient things of this world) shine in the light of the *voces* (the divine words as bearers of immutable truth), was the thematic preacher's ultimate goal.[28]

But grammar's content at the end of twefth century had not yet evolved into the grand theoretical edifices of the "modistae." Its incomplete metamorphosis spawned an eclecticism that was indifferent alike to the logical differentiation of necessary and probable arguments and to the theological limitation of persuasion to profound and salubrious truths, yet willing to learn and borrow from both. The process was epitomized in the "moderni," who professed a concern for practical issues and effective

---

[24] Paul Vignaux, *Philosophy in the Middle Ages* (London: Burns and Oates, 1959), 7 and John Marenbon, "The Twelfth Century," in *Medieval Philosophy*, ed. John Marenbon (London: Routledge, 1998), 180.

[25] Philotheus Boehner, *Medieval Logic* (Manchester: Manchester University Press, 1952), 15; see also *The Cambridge History of Later Medieval Philosophy*, ed. Norman Kretzman *et al.* (Cambridge, Eng.: Cambridge University Press, 1982), 315. The techniques employed in *disputatio* are carefully explained in John Marenbon's *Later Medieval Philosophy* (London: Routledge and Kegan Paul, 1981), 12–14 and 19–25. My object in this section is to establish the climate in which the sermon manual could develop; I am well aware of David d'Avray's caveat about the relationship between logic and the arts of preaching, voiced in his *The Preaching of the Friars* (Oxford: Clarendon, 1985), 178: "Logic provided ready-made terminology for *describing* the practice of division, but that does not in itself prove that logic influenced its evolution."

[26] *The Cambridge History of Later Medieval Philosophy*, 322. In the fifteenth century Louis de Rocha identified *positio* as the first component of a sermon (MS. Munich 3865, fol. 86v). Forms of the verb *pono*, however, are commonplace in discussions of the theme from the earliest *artes praedicandi*.

[27] Thurot, *Notices et extraits*, 218 and *The Cambridge History of Later Medieval Philosophy*, 110. To understand how important *congruitas* was to sermon theorists, see John of Wales, *Tractatus de arte predicandi* (MS. Paris, Mazarine 569, fols. 81v–82r). A text remarkably similar to the *Tractatus* was printed in Ulm by Zainer in 1480 as part of the works of Albert the Great, a fate common to several putative copies of John's treatise. Others have been listed as anonymous.

[28] *The Cambridge History of Later Medieval Philosophy*, 89.

applications.[29] They were roundly attacked by the exponents of the "purer" arts: by logicians who called them sophists, by theologians who designated them the brethren of heretical dialacticians and garrulous ratiocinators, and by humanists like John of Salisbury, who made a certain Cornificius the butt of some of the more scornful passages in the *Metalogicon*.[30] For the "moderni," the rules of dialectic were not to be regarded as infallible; likewise, visionary theory and inapplicable generalization in theology were devoid of moral attraction. Consequently, they focused on actions and words and their doctrine took shape, not in controversy and theoretical formulas, but in textbooks such as the *artes praedicandi*. Because these works put philosophy in the service of an apostolate and because grammar's metamorphosis allowed for such a practical outcome, by 1275 the term "moderni" was used to describe thematic sermon theorists; their method was called "modernorum."[31]

III.

The third element which fostered the creation of *artes praedicandi* can be identified within the preaching tradition itself. In the monasteries, the progressive transformation of the ancient homily into the thematically developed medieval sermon proceeded irregularly between 1050 and 1200, although preachers like William of Flay, Thomas of Morigny, Lambert of Belgium, Foulques of Neuilly, and even Bernard of Clairvaux carried forward with increasing momentum the organization of sermon matter.[32] The status of monastic preaching in the later twelfth century can be demonstrated from the prologue of Peter of Cornubia's *Panteologus*; there he describes a homily delivered by Gilbert Foliot at a synod attended by himself and by Stephen, Prior of Holy Trinity, Aldgate.[33] Peter could not restrain his praise of and admiration for

---

[29] Richard McKeon, "Rhetoric in the Middle Ages," *Speculum* 17 (1942), 1–32, at 26–7: "Gradually, in the course of the twelfth and thirteenth centuries they limited their statements to figures and forms of words, accomplishing their practical objectives by that device in a fashion which met with little effective opposition from logicians and theologians, and since they were unhampered by the need to consider things or thoughts, they were prolific in production of 'new' methods — they were fond of calling themselves 'moderni' …"

[30] John of Salisbury, *Metalogicon*, ed. Clement Webb (Oxford: Clarendon, 1929), 5.

[31] In the Ulm version of John of Wales' *Tractatus*, references to "moderni" begin on fol. 17v.

[32] Margaret Jennings, "*Non ex virgine*: The Rise of the Thematic Sermon Manual," *Collegium Medievale* 1–2 (1992), 27–44, at 36–7 and Jean Leclercq, "Le sermon sur la royauté du Christ au moyen âge," *Archives d'histoire doctrinale et littéraire du moyen âge* 15 (1943), 143–80, at 162–3 and 171.

[33] Peter does not date the synod, but it is known that Stephen was Prior of Holy Trinity in the latter part of the twelfth century, ca. 1170–97. See Richard W. Hunt, "English Learning in the Late Twelfth Century," *Transactions of the Royal Historical Society* 19 (1936), 19–42, at 33–4.

Gilbert's address because it was clearly formulated, varied by certain distinctions, adorned with flowers of words and sentences, and supported by a copious array of authorities; indeed, when Gilbert spoke of Christ as *petrus*, Peter reports, he used a three-pronged *distinctio* as a basis for his divisions: the stone which the builders had rejected, the stone which Jacob had set up as a pillar, and the stone that was cut out of a mountain without the agency of human hands.[34] But Foliot's effort is only one among many; as the thirteenth century dawned, monk preachers were, throughout Europe, systematically and successfully communicating the Word.

Providing an impetus toward thematic construction was not just the province of the monasteries; the influence of both university and cathedral sermonizing merits consideration in this regard. In the extra-monastic setting, however, the dividing line between patristic and thematic homiletics is both clearer and later. Paul Bonnes makes a good case for typing Geoffrey of Bath as the last patristic by juxtaposing his sermons with those of Peter Comestor.[35] But several other preachers could be placed in the Comestor orbit. Hilduin's structuralizing tendencies are well illustrated in his homily on Psalm 44, verse 11: "Tres legimus caelestis verbi auditores pigros, activos, contemplativos. Pigri torpent, activi laborant, contemplativi quiescunt..."[36] Peter of Poitiers thundered: "Triplex est generatio corruptionis, adoptionis, glorificationis" with the emphasis placed heavily on the first.[37] Probably the most organized and widely known of the Parisian Chancellors was the scolding and prophetic reformer, Raoul Ardent, whose work conforms almost totally to what would later be called thematic design; phrases similar to "tria facit apostolus" and "tribus capitulis distinguitur haec lectio" echo again and again.[38]

At the nadir of the twelfth century and under its aegis, sermon structures embodied the rhetorical expertise and intellectual awareness of their practitioners. But preachers did not just internalize and then set in motion a kind of amorphous *Zeitgeist*. They were encouraged, even impelled, toward schematization by the popular *Summa de arte predicatoria* of Alain de Lille.[39]

---

[34] For the Latin text, see Hunt, "English Learning," 41.

[35] See Jean Paul Bonnes, "Un des plus grands prédicateurs du XIIe siècle," *Revue Bénédictine* 56 (1945), 174–215.

[36] Johann B. Schneyer, *Repertorium der lateinischen Sermones des Mittelalters*, vol. 3, Beiträge zur Geschichte der Philosophie und Theologie des Mittelalters 43 (Münster: Aschendorff, 1970), 717.

[37] Jean Longère, *Œuvres oratoires des maîtres parisiens au XIIe siècle* (Paris: Études Augustiniennes, 1975), 56.

[38] Ibid., 57 and Jennings, "*Non ex virgine*," 39.

[39] PL 210, 110-98. A fine discussion of this text can be found in Marianne G. Briscoe, *Artes Praedicandi* (Turnhout: Brepols, 1992), pp. 20-25.

Alain's views on sermon composition were very clear. In the first place he defined the *quid sit* and *qualis sit* of preaching and signified its final cause as *informationi hominum deserviens*; he continued with a disposition-like formula for the sermon proper, indicating that its beginning should be taken from a theologically authoritative text, specifically the Gospels, Psalms, Pauline epistles, and the Wisdom literature; he advised that the preacher capture the good will of his hearers by the humility of his life, the utility of his preaching, and the attractiveness of qualities he proclaimed desirable; he counseled the preacher to adhere to *auctoritas* in the exposition of his sermon, although too abstruse a confirmation or too frequent a use of the sayings of the Gentiles must also be avoided; finally he acknowledged that the preacher may wish to move his audience to tears (*sed non nimis*) and use exempla (*ad probandum quod intendit*).[40]

It is tempting to seize upon this schema as the first *ars praedicandi,* although the text's brevity and virtual burial within Alain's whole *Summa* would seem to negate any such ascription.[41] Nevertheless, the bulk of this treatise (96%) — constituted of model sermons which correspond to the initial prescription detailed above — surely had an impact on preaching. The section entitled *Contra Accediam*, for example, is highly schematized. *Accedia* is described as that which causes the Christian to take his hand from the plow, as that which led Lot's wife to look back, as Ruth's reluctance to return to Bethlehem, as the monk's tepidity, the fellow of lust, the nurse of other vices, and so forth. Since the believer must rise from sleep (as counselled in Ephesians 5), three types of dreams are discussed, together with the scriptural authority relevant to the discussion; also, three types of sleep are treated. Finally, Scripture cries *Surge* "per rationis circumspectionem, per mali aspernationem, per boni operationem" and one rises "a terra in coelum, ab otio ad exercitum, a pernicioso torpore ad virtutes."[42] The treatise ends with a brief and organized discussion of the *quod* and *quibus* of preaching. Since Alain intended his *Summa* to be "not a fine art, but a useful art," [43]and since his model sermons were doubtless the verbatim source of many homiletic endeavors, his work is the last and a very strong impetus within the preaching tradition toward thematic form.

A coalescence of forces — principally exemplified by Ciceronian *dispositio*, grammatical metamorphosis, and schematized preaching — is proximately responsible for

---

[40] See PL 210, 111–14.

[41] Briscoe, *Artes Praedicandi*, 25, claims that Alain's *Summa* is "the first complete preaching manual" and the "most accomplished example of the genre." Jennings, "*Non ex virgine*," 39, discusses the small compass of the prescriptive sections of this treatise.

[42] PL 210, 125–8. There are about one hundred surviving manuscripts of Alain's *Summa*; see Guy Raynaud de Lage, *Alain de Lille* (Montreal: Institut d'études médiévales, 1951), 179–80.

[43] Gillian R. Evans, *Alan of Lille: The Frontiers of Theology in the Later Twelfth Century* (Cambridge, Eng.: Cambridge University Press, 1983), 101.

the development of the *artes praedicandi*. But no force exists in a vacuum. Behind the Ciceronian revival lay profound changes in the process of education; behind the evolution of grammar lay stupendous reworkings of the structure of thought; behind the interest in preaching lay the various ecclesiastical directives promulgated by the Third Council of the Lateran (1179) which initiated the process of grassroots evangelization. Peripheral to, yet exerting an influence on these movements was the growth of heresy in the later twelfth century;[44] certainly the Waldensians advocated and practiced frequent and efficacious preaching much to the distress of ecclesiastical authorities.

Superseding all of the above, however, and functioning as the overarching reasons for the rise of the *artes praedicandi* are several canons issuing from the Fourth Council of the Lateran (1215).[45] They and concomitant synodal constitutions fostered a great pastoral awakening which affected every area of the *cura animarum* and resulted in the composition of a myriad of pastoral treatises, including several arts of preaching. Chobham's led the way; William of Auvergne's developed procedures for expanding themes that would exemplify the power of God's word; Albert of Tortona's discussed exposition, division, and dilation; Richard of Thetford's elaborated eight modes of amplifying a sermon; John of La Rochelle's explicated rules for division and subdivision, as well as amplification; Humbert of Roman's stressed, somewhat idealistically, the elevated status of the preaching office.[46] Other than Chobham's — and perhaps because his text was not widely disseminated — no one of these manuals comprehensively incorporated classical dispositional structures; though informative about sermonizing in the early and mid-thirteenth century, they reflect only partially the prescriptive dynamic found in Cicero's early work and the *Rhetorica ad Herennium*.

---

[44] Malcolm Lambert, *Medieval Heresy* (Oxford: Blackwell, 1992) discusses the relevant theses and their proponents; see especially pp. 67–91 and Beverly Mayne Kienzle, "Holiness and Obedience: Denouement of Twelfth-Century Waldensian Lay Preaching," in *The Devil, Heresy and Witchcraft in the Middle Ages*, ed. Alberto Ferreiro (Leiden: Brill, 1998), 259–78. The *Patrologia Latina* contains several texts "contra hereticos"; see PL 210, 377–80 and 204, 812–16, among many others. For an overview of the shifts in thinking which characterized the period, see Harald Kleinschmidt, *Understanding the Middle Ages: The Transformation of Ideas and Attitudes in the Medieval World* (Rochester, NY: Boydell Press, 2000).

[45] The rise and development of pastoral attitudes in the Middle Ages is comprehensively surveyed in Fr. Leonard Boyle's unpublished D. Phil. dissertation, *A Survey of the Writings Attributed to William of Pagula*, vol. 1 (Oxford University, 1956). Other relevant sources will be noted below.

[46] See Jean Longère, *La prédication médiévale* (Paris: Études augustiniennes, 1983), 197–200; Franco Morenzoni, *Des écoles aux paroisses* (Paris: Études augustiniennes, 1995), 222–34; Briscoe, *Artes Praedicandi*, 30–6, and Morenzoni, "Parole," 279–83.

IV.

The inconsistencies which characterized the initial phase in the development of the *artes praedicandi* may have resulted from some obvious contradictions: Briscoe cites their position as "rhetorical treatises set within a devotional movement"; equally antithetical is their posited university locus, since Ciceronian rhetoric was hardly predominant in that venue by 1275.[47] Nevertheless, because rhetorical instruction seems to have retained its currency at other levels of education, the shaping spirit of the *De inventione* came to exert significant influence on the arts of preaching composed between the late thirteenth century and 1350. In their recommended sermon design, the theme — or scriptural text to be expounded — had, of course, no classical counterpart; however, a sermon's initial sections (protheme, prayer, and introduction) related to the Ciceronian *exordium*, the theme's exposition to *narratio*, its division to *partitio*, and its multifaceted amplification to *confirmatio*. The texts with this perceivably dispositional orientation are mostly of English provenance, namely: the *Tractatus de arte praedicandi* of John of Wales (ca. 1275), the *Forma praedicandi* of Robert of Basevorn (1322), the *De modo componendi sermones* of Thomas Waleys, who was still alive in 1349 but whose treatise is thought to come from the decade previous, and the *Ars componendi sermones* of Ranulph Higden (probably 1346).

John of Wales' manual contains a clear description of what he terms the best and most difficult species of sermon; it has theme, antetheme, prayer, repetition of the theme, introduction, division (plus confirmation) and subdivision (plus confirmation). John also provides a detailed explanation of ways of constructing the different parts of a sermon and a discussion of the appropriate adaptations of sermon to audience.[48] However, John of Wales' treatise is comparatively short (approximately eleven small folios); the longer texts — Robert of Basevorn's *Forma praedicandi* and Thomas Waleys'

---

[47] Marianne G. Briscoe, "How Was the *Ars Praedicandi* Taught in England?" in *The Uses of Manuscripts in Literary Studies*, ed. Charlotte Cook Morse (Kalamazoo: Medieval Institute Publications, 1992), 41–58, at 52. Although she maintains that they were not taught but were "contemporary responses to contemporary needs" (51), there is enough evidence to support the contention that those preaching manuals exemplifying Ciceronian *dispositio* emanate from a sub-university level of education, the schools of theology or "arts," located originally in Franciscan and Dominican convents and later in houses of several different orders; see Margaret Jennings, "Rhetor Redivivus: Cicero in the *Artes Praedicandi*," *Archives d'histoire doctrinale et littéraire du moyen âge* 16 (1989), 91–122, at 113–19. Ciceronian rhetoric maintained some presence in university venues; see John O. Ward, "Rhetoric in the Faculty of Arts at the Universities of Paris and Oxford in the Middle Ages," *Archivum Latinitatis Medii Aevi* 54 (1996), 159–232.

[48] Briscoe, *Artes Praedicandi*, 36–7, discusses several aspects of the *Tractatus*; see also Morenzoni, *Des écoles*, 235–6. John's longer works have been studied by Jenny Swanson, *John of Wales* (Cambridge, Eng.: Cambridge University Press, 1989).

De modo componendi sermones — elaborate on the John of Wales' structure with the exception of the protheme or antetheme, which Thomas virtually ignores in his chapter headings and which Robert subsumes into his criteria for choosing themes. John of Wales' discussion of appropriate adaptation of sermon to situation is given a prominent place in the later treatises and the originally classical concern about the qualities necessary in the preacher assumes great importance. It seems as if Cicero's fear that an orator's life might undermine his words had been internalized by Robert and Thomas; the first and quite extensive sections of their works are devoted to this aspect of the art of rhetoric. In terms of total plan, though, Waleys' text assumes the middle position; it is more formal and better organized than Basevorn's and proceeds, in nine sections, to discuss theme, prayer, introduction, division, and "prosecution," with an extra chapter on caveats and commonalities in divisions of theme.[49] Higden's *Ars* is more ordered still. Its clarity and conciseness act as a foil to Basevorn's tendency to attenuate his explanations.

Illustrative of this point are the sections dealing with the theme in the *Forma praedicandi* and the *Ars componendi sermones*. Basevorn, in chapters 15 through 23, discusses the nature of the theme and stresses that it be suitable, biblical, and divisible (the antetheme is mentioned here as a kind of afterthought); in chapter 26 he returns to a consideration of the biblical books where themes are commonly found; in chapters 27–30 he works again with themes, first commenting on those with scriptural and liturgical suitability, and then continuing to examples of themes for saints, on the necessity for having prepared sermons, and finally to incidental themes.[50] In the intervening chapters (24 and 25), Basevorn had considered ways of winning over the audience and the nature of prayers; the latter is a real hodge-podge, which Murphy's distillation makes abundantly clear:

> To me it seems good to propose the theme and to immediately make a prayer about it. I have not seen it mentioned in any genuine author that such a prayer ought to be said before the theme. Yet I have frequently seen it done. It is proper in either place, since both theme and prayer belong at the beginning. It should also be noted here that the prayer which is at the end of the antetheme ought always to depend upon what has preceded, so that it contains something which pertains to the prayer and at the same time contains a word of the theme even vocally, and especially that word on which depends the persuasion to prayer; this is the method of the Oxonians.[51]

---

[49] The arts of Thomas and Robert have been published in Th. Charland, *Artes praedicandi* (Ottawa: Publications de l'Institut d'études médiévales d'Ottawa, 1936); the *De modo componendi sermones* is found on pp. 327–403 and the *Forma praedicandi* on pp. 233–323.

[50] Murphy's *Rhetoric in the Middle Ages*, 344-55, contains a detailed outline of Basevorn's *Forma.*

[51] Ibid., 349.

As if he had realized the confusing aspects of the previous fifteen chapters, Basevorn begins chapter 31 by assuring his readers that he will return to the order set out in chapter 14!

By comparison, Higden's treatment of this material is a paradigm of orderly progression. He discusses the requirements for a suitable theme (chapter six), its relevance to occasion and audience (chapter seven), the necessity for biblical accuracy in choosing themes, coupled with the recognition that some insignificant omissions or additions can occur (chapter eight); chapter nine stresses the importance of the factor of sufficient divisibility in themes, while ten concentrates on the various types of parallel passages which can support themes. In chapter eleven, Higden moves gracefully to the extraction of prothemes, outlining several usable methods but noting that this section could be omitted if its prolixity impairs the effectiveness of the whole. Chapter twelve explains the intercessory prayer and thirteen outlines modes of insuring a favorable attitude in the audience.[52] At this distance it is difficult to say what importance the last named chapter has in its present position in Ranulph's text, but a conservative opinion might allow that winning audiences was not, in Ranulph's mind, a haphazard effort; rather, it was integral both to the development of a theme and its future prosecution.

The Higden/Basevorn differences, however, are not just confined to the characteristics of a theme: while Basevorn's *Forma* trails off into some seventeen methods of developing sermons and seven modes of "beautifying" them,[53] Ranulph proceeds in an organized fashion through division of a theme, divisional keys, dilation (or amplification) in general, subdivision, dilation through authorities, other rules for dilation, and rhetorical coloration.[54] Unlike Basevorn, who has difficulty in defining rhetorical terms accurately (for example, he calls introduction, division, and confirmation "ornaments" to a theme[55]), Ranulph is consistently able to characterize each point in his treatise, often using language very similar to that of the classical text. A case in point is his expectation that "auditores reddat benivoles et attentos ad audiendum et sollicitos ad exequendum" (his audience become willing and attentive listeners and concerned about

---

[52] *The Ars componendi sermones of Ranulph Higden*, ed. Margaret Jennings (Leiden: E. J. Brill, 1991), 15–34.

[53] Basevorn intertwines structural with ornamental procedures, thus Chapter 39: Amplification; Chapter 40: Subdivision; Chapter 41: Digression; Chapter 42: Correspondence. See Murphy, *Rhetoric in the Middle Ages*, 352–5.

[54] See *The Ars componendi sermones of Ranulph Higden*, 43–72. Subdivision was sometimes discussed under dilation or amplification, possibly because of the variable placement of proof permitted by the *Ad Herennium*. See Jennings, "*Rhetor Redivivus*," 93 and Jennings, "*Non ex virgine*," 31–2.

[55] "Et nunc ... expedito aliqualiter de tribus ornamentis antethematis (pro)sequendum est de ornamentis thematis, quorum primum est introductio" (Charland, *Artes praedicandi*, 268).

following the argument), which is remarkably close to Cicero's definition of the *exordium.*[56] It is even somewhat amusing that Basevorn, whose verbosity might have caused "Tully" some distress, makes four specific references to the "rhetoric" of Cicero and Pseudo-Cicero[57] while Ranulph does not invoke either name.[58]

Although all of the *artes praedicandi* provide extensive instructions to the preacher, their prescriptions are sometimes buried within elaborate discussions of contemporary intellectual issues. Ranulph Higden avoids such distractions, neither meandering into theological quagmires nor exploring material tangential to his purpose. In its clarity and conciseness, his *Ars componendi sermones* is balm to the misery of anyone who has ever suffered through a verbose diatribe on current moral lapses. Indeed, its easily followed organizational pattern and its admonition that a preacher shun wearisome wordiness[59] is surprising to those who look askance at sermonizing in any era, particularly the medieval one. Ranulph's directness may, of course, result from personal preference; more likely it springs from his extensive experience as a chronicler, both of world history and of the interests of the fourteenth-century church.

V.

Certainly Higden's greatest literary memorial is the *Polychronicon,* a universal history which gave to the learned people of fourteenth-century England a clear and original picture of events formative of their era; the work is based on medieval tradition but with a new interest in antiquity and with the early history of Britain related as part of

---

[56] See *De inventione,* 1.15.20 and *The Ars componendi,* 32. The first section of chapter 13 below contextualizes this statement. It is noteworthy that Ranulph preserves the term "auditores," which can refer to the congregation as well as to the principals in a legal procedure.

[57] In chapters 41, 45, and 50; see Charland, *Artes praedicandi,* 297, 305, 320.

[58] Two other names not invoked in this introduction are Ramon Llull and James of Fusignano. The former's art of preaching, which was translated into Latin in 1303, uses "sequences of allegorical interpretations to combine commonplace precepts with traditional moral instruction," according to Mark D. Johnston, "The *Rhetorica nova* of Ramon Llull: An *Ars praedicandi* as Devotional Literature," in *De Ore Domini,* ed. Thomas Amos *et al.* (Kalamazoo: Medieval Institute Publications, 1989), 119–45, at 119. Johnston refines his vision of Llull's treatise in *The Evangelical Rhetoric of Ramon Llull* (New York: Oxford, 1996), 27, calling it "a work of moral literature on speech." James of Fusignano's *Libellus de arte predicandi* (ca. 1300) generally follows Ciceronian formats, but skews its commentary toward dilation by devoting 75% of the text to this process. See Jennings, "Rhetor," 100–01. Franco Morenzoni, "Parole," 285–7, is more sympathetic to Fusignano's work than I am, noting especially its widespread dissemination.

[59] See *The Ars componendi,* 14.

the whole.[60] From the chronicle of Henry Knighton, canon of Leicester abbey, one learns that Higden thought to bring his *Polychronicon* to an end in 1327 but later continued it to 1340.[61] Huntington Library MS. 132 bears witness to this later composition; it is generally considered the working copy of the last and fullest recension of the text, written most likely in 1340 and added to for several years afterwards.[62] Of particular interest here is Higden's practice in quoting from his authorities; he does not generally copy their words verbatim but rather gives the sense with an accuracy which makes for quick spotting of corrupt textual transmission.[63] Higden's superlative comprehension of his sources, his demonstrably painstaking procedure for surveying numerous historical epochs, the length of time required for the *Polychronicon*'s completion, and its obvious thoroughness may be sufficient explanations for its pre-Reformation popularity.[64] Even the most cursory survey of this text, however, convinces one that "Higden's mind was set chiefly on completeness and he is better described as an encyclopedist than a historian proper."[65]

The characterization, "encyclopedist," applies also with great accuracy to his other writings, which are more overtly religious than the *Polychronicon* and which were in Tanner's words "sui temporis laude digna."[66] Certainly Higden's reputation was responsible for the spurious identification of him as the playwright of the Chester Corpus Christi plays; likewise spurious is his supposed authorship of a long sermon manuscript whose *incipit* reads "cum in ecclesia mea quietus residerem et loquendi ad populum."[67] Among those works which are likely to be Ranulph's are lists of *distinctiones theologicae*, expositions of Job and the Canticle of Canticles, an *Ars kalendarii*, and a *Pedagogium artis grammaticae*.[68] The last is no longer extant, although it did at one time form

[60] The text has been studied by John Taylor, *The Universal Chronicle of Ranulph Higden* (Oxford: Clarendon, 1966). A nine-volume edition of the *Polychronicon* was published in the Rolls Series, the first two respectively in 1865 and 1869 under the editorship of Canon Hardwick and Churchill Babington, the last seven volumes under the editorship of James R. Lumby in 1886.

[61] V. H. Galbraith, "An Autograph MS. of Ranulph Higden's *Polychronicon*," *The Huntington Library Quarterly* 23 (1959), 1–18, at 1.

[62] Ibid., 5.

[63] Ibid., 17.

[64] Jennings, "Higden's Minor Writings," 151.

[65] Galbraith, "Autograph," 17.

[66] Thomas Tanner, *Bibliotheca Britannica Hibernica* (London: Gulielmus Bowyer, 1748), 402–03.

[67] Moses Tyson, in his "Handlist of Additions to the Collections of Latin Manuscripts in the John Rylands Library, 1908–1928," *Bulletin of the John Rylands Library* 12 (1928), 581–609, at 600, had identified Ranulph as the author of MS. 367. The ascription was corrected (in personal correspondence with me, May 9, 1969) by Dr. F. Taylor, then Keeper of Manuscripts at the John Rylands Library; Ralph Acton is undoubtedly the preacher in question.

[68] Taylor, *The Universal Chronicle*, 182–4.

part of the library of Syon abbey and its composition is certainly in line with the Benedictine emphasis on education which came into even greater prominence after the reforms of Benedict XII.[69] The other works, and an *Abbreviationes chronicorum*, are said to be Higden's by both secular and Benedictine bibliographers and it is probable, in the light of his historical and theological labors, that these attributions or references to similar works are substantially correct.[70] In fact, the *Ars kalendarii*, which forms part of Magdalene College Cambridge MS. 23, reflects Higden's concerns both in style and content.[71] Its *explicit* even underlines his encyclopaedist tendencies, since he claims to have compiled ("compilavi" his own work in order to instruct those untutored in the computational complexities of reckoning time using, for this purpose, the well-known authors "dionisium exiguum, bedam, elpericum, ptolomeum, al-faraganum" along with a few near contemporaries.[72] That the treatise preceding the *Ars kalendarii* in the manuscript (as it is currently bound) could readily be one from which Ranulph had "gathered" material is curiously à propos.

Despite the fact that monks were generally prohibited from exercising the care of souls in the thirteenth and early fourteenth centuries,[73] Higden's *Speculum curatorum* and *Ars componendi sermones* situate him not only within the widening stream of fourteenth-century church life, but also within the ever developing pastoral renewal which was its driving force. The *Speculum* is one of many manuals created, in light of

---

69 *Catalogue of the Library of Syon Monastery, Isleworth*, ed. Mary Bateson (Cambridge, Eng.: The University Press, 1898), 2.

70 See Magnoaldo Ziebelbauer, *Historia rei literariae ordinis S. Benedicti* (Vienna: M. Veith, 1754), vol. 4, pp. 30, 40, 113, 162, 323, 334, 466, and 655.

71 See MS. Cambridge, Magdalene College 23, fols. 23v–36r. Tables follow on fols. 36v, 37v, and 38; the recto of fol. 37 is blank.

72 Ibid., fol. 36r. The people mentioned here had reputations for various computational ventures in the Middle Ages: Dionysius Exiguus had prepared an Easter table following Alexandrian principles; Bede and Helperic of Auxerre used empirical methodology to confirm the dates of solstices and equinoxes; al-Farghani presented numerical values, based on Ptolemy's model of the nested planetary spheres, for the dimensions of the universe. See Stephen McCluskey, *Astronomies and Culture in Early Medieval Europe* (Cambridge, Eng.: Cambridge University Press, 1998), 87, 150–2, and 189.

73 See Margaret Jennings, "Monks and the *Artes Praedicandi* in the Time of Ranulph Higden," *Revue Bénédictine* 86 (1976), 119–28. Joan Greatrex theorizes that Ranulph's pastoral works may have been composed in response to an expressed need among local parish clergy; she maintains that there are "insufficient grounds for claiming Higden's productions as evidence of a need to train monks to fill vacant parishes, or for interpreting them as the sign of a change of direction among Benedictines vis-à-vis their monastic vocation"; see Joan Greatrex, "Benedictine Sermons: Preparation and Practice in the English Monastic Cathedral Cloisters," in *Medieval Monastic Preaching*, ed. Carolyn Muessig (Leiden: Brill, 1998), 257–78, at 275.

the mandates of the Fourth Council of the Lateran (1215), to aid those practicing the *cura animarum* by explicating for them every element of parochial instruction (prayer, the sacraments, the vices and virtues). As its *incipit* indicates, Higden's handbook is a compilation and acquires much of its content from the common sources of material for members of this genre.[74] It probably owes a little to the *Manipulus curatorum* of Henry of Ghent,[75] but it is generally dependent on the *Summa confessorum* of John of Freiburg, which it periodically transcribes verbatim, and upon the *Oculus sacerdotis* of William of Pagula, which it uses without acknowledgement for points concerning occasional preaching and excommunication.[76] Higden's pastoral manual, like its many predecessors, is an outcome of Fourth Lateran's prodigious ecclesiastical effort to educate both clergy and laity, an effort unparalleled until Vatican II. Although it boasts some amusing explanations of church practices (for example, in its contorted explanations about the congruence between the twelve apostles and the Apostles' Creed[77]) and makes several contributions to our understanding of fourteenth-century culture (especially in the chapter on *sortilegium*[78]), the real nature of Higden's *Speculum* cannot be defined through individual chapters but must be sought in its function as a "mirror for curates." If the work illustrates that Ranulph was at home with the lore of constellations, the properties of things, the psychology of dreams, and some of the typical medieval sources of popular habits and ideals, it shows this as part of Higden's pastoral

[74] The "compilavi" of the *explicit* to the *Ars Kalendarii* is echoed in the acrostic of the *Speculum*. Even a cursory glance at notes to manuals like the *Summa confessorum* and the *Memoriale presbyterorum* will show how commonly used some sources, like John of Freiburg, were. Thomas Chobham's *Summa*, despite its title, is a manual about pastoral care in general; it has been edited by F. Broomfield in Analecta Medievalia Namurcensia 25 (Louvain: Nauwelaerts, 1968). The *Memoriale*, which is more properly a confessor's manual, has been edited by Michael Haren and extensively studied in his *Sin and Society in Fourteenth-Century England* (Oxford: Oxford University Press, 2000). Extant manuscripts of the *Speculum curatorum* are London, British Library Harley 1004; Oxford, Balliol 77; Cambridge, Univ. Lib. Mm.i.20; Durham B.iv.36; and University of Illinois 251/H53s.

[75] Ranulph uses one of these quodlibets on fol. 98v of the Balliol College manuscript; see the note in Boyle, *A Survey*, 303.

[76] "Secundum Thomam" is the usual introduction to a citation from John of Freiburg. Higden gets his topics for occasional preaching, as well as his listing of excommunications, from Pagula; see Jennings, "Higden's Minor Writings," 157, note 41.

[77] See "De articulis fidei," in MS. Balliol College 77, fols. 3v–4r. Ranulph mentions several ways of dividing up the fourteen credal statements and then decides to assign the first three to Peter.

[78] See G. R. Owst, "*Sortilegium* in English Homiletic Literature of the Fifteenth Century," in *Studies Presented to Sir Hilary Jenkinson*, ed. J. C. Davies (London: Oxford University Press, 1957), 272–303. Other amusing aspects of the *Speculum* (notably the chapters "De ludificationibus demonum" and "De gradibus peccatorum") have been treated by Eugene Crook and Margaret Jennings in "The Devil and Ranulph Higden," *Manuscripta* 22 (1978), 131–40 and "Grading Sin: A Medieval English Benedictine in the *Cura animarum*," *The American Benedictine Review* 31 (1980), 335–45.

effort, of his endeavor to bring the tenets of the great canon lawyers and theologians into the purview of the parish priest, as well as into the ambit of the ordinary layman who needed instruction in a faith that was no longer wholly simple, no longer able to be blindly accepted.

Unlike the *Speculum* (where the chapters' initial letters read seriatim *Cestrensis monachus Ranulphus compilavit hoc speculum anno Domini MCCC quadragesimo*[79]), the *Ars componendi sermones* (whose chapter initials spell *Ars Ranulphi Cestrensis*) is not assigned a specific year. Critical opinion, however, seems agreed that the acrostic scheme came as an afterthought to Ranulph, probably about 1340.[80] Because the *terminus ad quem* of the holograph copy of the *Polychronicon* is post-1340, it seems likely that the *Ars* was written afterward and probably as late as 1346. Several factors may have encouraged its composition around this time: acknowledgement of the desirable aspects of pastoral functioning even for English Black monks at the chapters of 1336, 1343, and 1346; emphasis upon university influence in the monasteries, which only began in earnest after the reforms of 1336 and which probably took a few years to penetrate to Chester; conditions in Ranulph's own monastery, which may well have encouraged him in more religious pursuits than the compilation of a universal history; increase in the number of priests instituted to ordination through the monastery, a task for which some of the brethren must have felt a responsibility; finally, the exemption of monastic advowsons from episcopal control and the probable monkish *cura* practiced in those places which were beyond the bishop's jurisdiction.[81] It is reasonable to assume, moreover, that Ranulph, having produced a long and detailed manual for the use of the parish priest in the instruction of his flock, would also feel obliged to help that same parson organize the content of his sermons into an intelligible and forceful whole. If this were so, Higden would be following in the footsteps of such manualists as Alan of Lille, Robert Grosseteste, Thomas Chobham, John of Wales, Aestanus of Asti, John of Erfurt, Bartholomew of Pisa, Nicolas of Ausimo, Henry of Langenstein, and Jean Gerson, who wrote *artes praedicandi* in addition to their penitential and doctrinal works.[82] That Ranulph's penchant for organization and compilation should have

---

79 The Illinois manuscript of the *Speculum* does not preserve the acrostic structure. See Eugene Crook, "A New Version of Ranulph Higden's *Speculum Curatorum*," *Manuscripta* 21 (1977), 41–9.

80 Jennings, "Higden's Minor Writings," 153.

81 The great decline in Chester began with the abbacy of the violent Richard of Seynesbury (1349–62), a period which encompasses the final quarter of Higden's life. See Jennings, "Higden's Minor Writings," 153 and 156, note 15.

82 Useful commentary on these authors and texts can be found in Pierre Michaud-Quantin, *Sommes de casuistique et manuels de confession au moyen âge* (Montreal: Librairie dominicaine, 1962), 16, 54, 57, 60, 77, 81, and *passim* on the *Templum Domini* of Robert Grosseteste.

come into play in this fashion would certainly be congruent with his previous efforts in the *Polychronicon* and the *Speculum*.

Higden's *Ars* explicates briefly and clearly the conventions for devising thematic or scholastic sermons: in essence they mandate that, having chosen a biblical theme and extended its significance in a protheme, the preacher is to introduce his theme in a specific manner, divide it tripartly, and embellish it suitably. Accordingly, through a preface and twenty concise chapters, Ranulph's text charts an almost foolproof course towards successful preaching in the thematic mode. Adherence to its precepts, the monk declares, should result in furthering the spread of divine worship, in enlightening the church militant, and in inflaming mankind's love for God.[83] Having rejected sermonizing that is either strident or infelicitous, the *Ars componendi sermones* maintains that true preaching will be founded on the disciplined and practical use of Scripture as is, indeed, the treatise itself. The preface's demand that a parson possess correctness of intention, holiness of behavior, and aptitude for public speaking is developed in chapters II, III, and IV, where excellence in motive and example and maturity in style and presentation are emphasized. The preface's further development of sermon requisites, like consonance of theme with topic, propriety in division, and overall spiritual utility, forms the backdrop for most of the remaining chapters: five are devoted to theme, five to division and its concomitants, and four to sermon embellishment and audience appeal.

Formatted for the preacher's convenience, the twenty-one sections outline the major points to be stressed and the major pitfalls to be sidestepped in sermon construction. Logical progression is paramount and, though non-linear argumentation and the more subtle forms of linguistic analysis are explained, the preacher is counseled that these are not useful for ordinary people.[84] Apart from the advice which is peculiar to its use of the Latin language, areas common to sermon manuals in any age — rhetorical effectiveness, exemplary storytelling, scriptural accuracy, analytic lucidity — are treated in Higden's text. Of course, a delightful medieval bias is evident intermittently in the monk's acceptance of an allegorical signification for biblical names, in his scriptural exposition which allows for four senses usually identified as historical, tropological, allegorical, and anagogical, and in his care to distinguish the Parisian preaching patterns from those in use in Oxford.[85] Ranulph took advantage of medieval logic's readymade terminology for describing the practice of division by relating the (Aristotelian)

[83] *The Ars componendi*, 5.

[84] Ibid., 57. Explanations of non-linear argumentation and subtle forms of linguistic analysis form the core of chapter 17: "De sermonis dilatacione."

[85] The allegorical signification of biblical names is treated in chapter 20, the four senses of scriptural interpretation in chapters 14, 18, and 19, and the Paris/Oxford approaches to thematic form in chapter 12.

four causes to preaching, through his insistence that argumentative sermons should employ induction, syllogism, and enthymeme, and in discussing universals and particulars, genera and species, substance and accidents.[86] References to the monastic horarium, especially to elements of the Night and Day Offices — times of prayer which punctuated daily life at St. Werburgh's — also appear in the *Ars*.[87] But more important than all of these and chief among the text's obvious virtues is its clarity. By following its directions even the indifferent preacher would be able to create a semblance of the perfect "tree of preaching" which was the ideal of the thematic mode.[88]

Ranulph's *Ars* survives in five manuscript versions, four housed in Oxford's Bodleian Library and one at London's British Library; except for MS. Bodley 316, which reputedly dates from 1388, all are of the fifteenth century and no one of the five is directly transcribed from any of the others.[89] Two recensions of the text are bound into the same volume, MS. Bodley 5 (folios 1r–17r and 85v–102r).[90] Both seem to have been derived from similar models, although scribal variants and outright mistakes indicate that they were not copied from each other. MS. Bodley 5, which is the size of a modern paperback, would have been eminently portable, its working hand easily readable — a handy reference tool.

MS. Auctarium F.3.5, another Bodleian manuscript, is virtually square, measuring 10 and 7/8 inches in length and width.[91] The *Ars componendi sermones*, found on folios 9r to 25r, probably preserves Higden's original organization of the treatise in listing the acrostically significant chapter titles first and then proceeding immediately to the preface. However, the text's large number of syntactically impossible readings and its incorporation of seeming commentaries or glosses into the prescriptive sequences militates against granting it exemplar status.

MS. Bodley 316 is the most beautiful of the surviving manuscripts, written in double columns in a clear Gothic bookhand and boasting miniatures, illuminated

---

86 See below, chapter 18: "De membrorum subdivisione," and d'Avray, *The Preaching of the Friars*, 178.

87 Matins comprises the Night Office; the Day Office has seven components: Lauds, Prime, Terce, Sext, None, Vespers, and Compline. The timeline for these "hours" of prayer varied from summer to winter and because of local feasts. See David Knowles, *The Monastic Horarium* (Cambridge, Eng.: Cambridge University Press, 1941), 714.

88 See Otto Dieter, "*Arbor Picta*: The Medieval Tree of Preaching," *Quarterly Journal of Speech* 51 (1965), 123–44.

89 *The Ars componendi sermones of Ranulph Higden*, xli.

90 The manuscript is carefully described by Falconer Madden and H. H. E. Craster in their *A Summary Catalogue of Western Manuscripts in the Bodleian Library, Oxford*, vol. 2, part 1 (Oxford: Clarendon, 1932), 82; see also, *The Ars componendi*, xli. Briscoe, "How … Taught," 49, says that MS. Bodley 5 is an illustration of "a pechia copying system gone awry."

91 Madan and Craster, *A Summary Catalogue*, 492, and *The Ars componendi*, xliv–xlv.

92 Madan and Craster, *A Summary Catalogue*, 527–8, and *The Ars componendi*, xli–xlii.

borders, and decorated initials.[92] A large volume (15 inches by 10 and 5/8 inches), it is comprised of several different treatises, one of which is Higden's *Polychronicon*. The *Ars componendi sermones* is last, occupying folios 176r–83r.

The British Library's MS. Harley 866 is looseleaf size and contains a variety of treatises in different hands.[93] The *Ars componendi sermones* (here folios 8r –17r) was once part of another compilation. Especially interesting are its three hands: the transcriber's is a formal, minuscule bookhand, similar to the corrector's, and may preserve a kind of fifteenth century spellcheck! The marginal notations, however, are in a script quite different from the other two; they are written in a formal, square, literary hand in a lighter color ink. MS. Harley 866 was the copy text of the Latin edition of Higden's *Ars* from which this translation was made.

As in the *Polychronicon* and *Speculum*, Higden compiled his art of preaching from the many treatises on the subject available to him. Although some scholars have considered his text merely an abridgement of Robert of Basevorn's *Forma praedicandi*,[94] a careful analysis of its contents reveals obvious borrowings from the tripartite Franciscan *Ars concionandi*, the *Ars praedicandi* of John of Wales, the *Distinctiones* of Nicolas Byard, an extended treatment of Richard of Thetford's commentary on dilation, and Thomas Waley's *De modo componendi sermones*, as well as from Basevorn. Echoes of numerous other treatises are also discernible, especially in the chapters "De dicendi circumspeccione" and "De membrorum subdivisione."[95]

Ranulph's handling of his sources — selecting, integrating, facilitating the use of a previously developed matrix rather than creating a new one — prompts a few observations about his relationship with his age. Certainly, as historian, encyclopaedist, and developer of the *cura animarum*, he merits a place among the "worthies" of the medieval period. Yet, he was not a literary giant like the Pearl Poet, nor a visionary like Richard Rolle, nor even a commentator on his time like John Gower. Higden's genius lay in his knack of choosing and focusing the best of the past to meet the needs of the present. Trained in the Benedictine tradition of education and service, Ranulph became a transmitter of fact, of ideals, and of expertise. Unfortunately, the shining

[93] *The Catalogue of the Harleian Manuscripts in the British Museum*, vol. I (London: Eyre/Strahan, 1808), p. 463 and *The Ars componendi*, pp.xliii-xliv.

[94] This view was propagated by Th. Charland, Harry Caplan, and James J. Murphy. A summary statement is contained in James J. Murphy, "Rhetoric in Fourteenth-Century Oxford," *Medium Aevum* 34 (1965), 1–20, at 14. Recent reassessments of the function of copying in the Middle Ages seem to be reversing the previously negative judgment; Michael Haren comments: "We place such a heavy premium on originality that we are disposed to attend only to originality, an approach that can make us miss much of historical value in medieval compilation" (Letter to me, dated October 27, 2000).

[95] A detailed outline of Higden's *Ars*, showing its multiple and varied sources, is contained in *The Ars componendi*, 73–80.

achievements of this era's great thinkers have obscured his important function; the emblematic names of fourteenth-century England remain Wyclif, Langland, and Chaucer — and rightly so, for through them we are exposed to that epoch's theological innovations, its intellectual range, and its imaginative triumphs. But when one wants to reconstruct the background out of which such originality emerged, when one delves deeply enough to want a perspective on the material that Chaucer knew, and Langland criticized, and Wyclif wrestled with, then one must read Higden.

Selected Bibliography

General Overviews of subjects relevant to the *Art of Composing Sermons* and its author are contained in the *Dictionary of the Middle Ages*, ed. Joseph R. Strayer (New York: Charles Scribner's Sons, 1987). Most pertinent are the entries **Ars poetica**: 1, 553–55; **Ars praedicandi**: 1, 555–58; **Benedictines**: 2, 171–76; **Dictamen**: 4, 173–77; **Exegesis, Latin**: 4, 542–45; **Higden, Ranulph**: 6, 224; **Preaching and Sermon Literature**: 10, 75–82; **Rhetoric (W. European)**: 10, 351–64.

Also useful for general background is William Abel Pantin, *The English Church in the Fourteenth Century* (Cambridge, Eng.: Cambridge University Press, 1955).

The medieval pastoral movement, given impetus by the Third (1189) and Fourth (1215) Lateran Councils, emphasized the care of souls (*cura animarum*) of which preaching is an integral part; see Leonard E. Boyle, O. P., *A Survey of the Writings Attributed to William of Pagula*, D. Phil. Dissertation (Oxford, 1956) vol. 1. Fr. Boyle's ancillary studies of this phenomenon have been collected in *Pastoral Care, Clerical Education and Canon Law: 1200–1400* (London: Variorum Reprints, 1981). Related texts in English appear in *Pastors and the Care of Souls in Medieval England*, ed. John Shinners and William J. Dohar, Notre Dame Texts in Medieval Culture 4 (Notre Dame: Notre Dame University Press, 1998).

More detailed studies of Higden's time and text can be found in the following:

RANULPH HIGDEN, O.S.B. (Order of St. Benedict)

Benedictine Monasticism in the Middle Ages

Daly, Lowrie, *Benedictine Monasticism* (New York: Sheed and Ward, 1965).

Harvey, Barbara, *Living and Dying in England, 1100-1540: The Monastic Experience* (Oxford: Clarendon, 1993).

Leclercq, Jean, *The Love of Learning and the Desire for God*, trans. Catherine Misrahi (New York: Fordham University Press, 1961).

Leclercq, Jean *et al.*, *The Spirituality of the Middle Ages* (London: Burns and Oates, 1968).

Knowles, David, *The Religious Orders in England*, 2 vols. (Cambridge, Eng.: Cambridge University Press, 1948).

Knowles, David, *Christian Monasticism* (New York: McGraw-Hill, 1969).

Zarnecki, George, *The Monastic Achievement* (New York: McGraw-Hill, 1972).

The Monastery of St. Werburgh's (Chester Cathedral)

Bennett, F.S.M., *Chester Cathedral* (Chester: Phillipson and Golder, 1926).

Burne, R.V.H., *The Monks of Chester: The History of St. Werburgh's Abbey* (London: Society for the Preservation of Christian Knowledge, 1962).
Cranage, D.H.S., *The Home of the Monk* (Cambridge: The University Press, 1926).
Hiatt, Charles, *The Cathedral Church of Chester* (London: George Bell & Sons, 1897).
Jones, Douglas, *The Church in Chester, 1300–1540* (Manchester: Chetham Society, 1957).
Morris, Richard, *Cathedrals and Abbeys of England and Wales* (New York: Norton, 1979).
Pevsner, Nikolaus and Priscilla Metcalf, *The Cathedrals of England* (New York: Viking, 1985).
http://www.chestercathedral.org.uk

Higden's Life and Works

Crook, Eugene, "A New Version of Ranulph Higden's *Speculum Curatorum*," *Manuscripta* 21 (1977), 41–9.
Edwards, J. G., "Ranulph, Monk of Chester," *English Historical Review* 47 (1932), 94.
Galbraith, V. H., "An Autograph MS. of Ranulph Higden's *Polychronicon*," *The Huntington Library Quarterly* 23 (1959), 1–18.
Jennings, Margaret, "Monks and the *Artes praedicandi* in the Time of Ranulph Higden," *Revue Bénédictine* 86 (1976), 119–28.
—, "Higden's Minor Writings and the Fourteenth Century Church." *Proceedings of the Leeds Literary and Historical Society* 16 (1977), 149–58.
—, "The Preacher's Rhetoric: The *Ars componendi sermones* of Ranulph Higden," in *Medieval Eloquence*, ed. James J. Murphy (Berkeley: University of California Press, 1978), 114–26.
— and Eugene Crook, "The Devil and Ranulph Higden," *Manuscripta* 22 (1978), 131–40.
— and Eugene Crook, "Grading Sin: A Medieval English Benedictine in the *Cura animarum*," *American Benedictine Review* 31 (1980), 335–45.
— (ed.), *The Ars componendi sermones of Ranulph Higden, O.S.B.* (Leiden: E. J. Brill, 1991).
Taylor, John, *The Universal Chronicle of Ranulph Higden* (Oxford: Clarendon, 1966).

THE ARTES PRAEDICANDI AND RHETORICAL TRADITIONS

Classical Rhetoric

The relationship of the *Artes praedicandi* to elements of classical rhetoric has been explored at some length in the introduction. The ramifications of this topic are studied in:

Jennings, Margaret, "*Rhetor redivivus*: Cicero in the *Artes praedicandi*," *Archives d'histoire doctrinale et littéraire du moyen âge* 56 (1989), 91–122.

Medieval Rhetoric

In 1942, Richard McKeon challenged scholars to explore the many facets of "Rhetoric in the Middle Ages" (*Speculum* 17 [1942], 1–32). In splendid response to this challenge, James J. Murphy wrote at length about the origin and development of its many elements in *Rhetoric in the Middle Ages* (Berkeley: University of California Press, 1974).

Murphy's discussion of the *artes praedicandi* is both comprehensive and readable and its extensive footnotes are supplemented by his *Medieval Rhetoric: A Select Bibliography* (Toronto: University of Toronto Press, 1989). This bibliography provides information on the major contributors to the scholarly exploration of all three *artes*; for the art of preaching, the works of H. Caplan, M. T. d'Alverny, Th.-M. Charland, J. Longère, J. J. Murphy, G. R. Owst, D. Roth, and C. Smyth are particularly important. Those who benefit from graphic presentations should see Otto Dieter's "*Arbor picta*: the Medieval Tree of Preaching," *Quarterly Journal of Speech* 51 (1965), 123–44.

Pre-1974, James Murphy endeavored, through Leopold Krul's translation, to acquaint students with the content of a specific art of preaching — the *Forma praedicandi* of Robert of Basevorn — as well as with the scope of treatises describing the "sister" arts of poetry and letter writing. The resultant text, *Three Medieval Rhetorical Arts*, ed. James J. Murphy (Berkeley: University of California Press, 1971), is a convenient and useful introduction to these well-known members of the medieval rhetorical tradition.

In more recent publications, other scholars have approached these *artes* and their applications from many different vantage points. Some of the easily accessible studies of the *ars praedicandi* are:

Briscoe, Marianne G., *Artes Praedicandi* (Turnhout: Brepols, 1992).

—, "How was the *Ars praedicandi* Taught in England?" in *The Uses of Manuscripts in Literary Studies*, ed. Charlotte Cook Morse (Kalamazoo: Medieval Institute Publications, 1992), 115–21.

Jennings, Margaret, "*Non ex virgine*: The Rise of the Thematic Sermon Manual," *Collegium Medievale* 1–2 (1992), 27–44.

Johnston, Mark D., "The *Rhetorica nova* of Ramon Llull: An *Ars praedicandi* as Devotional Literature," in *De Ore Domini*, ed. Thomas Amos *et al.* (Kalamazoo: Medieval Institute Publications, 1989), 119–45.

Morenzoni, Franco, *Thomas Chobham: Summa de Arte Praedicandi* (Turnhout: Brepols, 1988).

—, "Aux origines des *Artes praedicandi*: *De artificioso modo predicandi* d'Alexandre d'Ashby," *Studii Medievali*, 3rd series, 32 (1991), 907–18.

—, *Des écoles aux paroisses: Thomas Chobham et la promotion de la prédication au début du XIIIe siècle* (Paris: Études Augustiniennes, 1995).

—, "La littérature des *Artes praedicandi* de la fin du XIIe au debut du XVe siècle." in *Sprachtheorien in Spätantike und Mittelalter*, ed. S. Ebbesen, Geschichte der Sprachtheorie 3 (Tübingen: Narr, 1995), 339–59.
—, "Parole du prédicateur et inspiration divine d'après les *Artes praedicandi*," in *La parole du prédicateur, V–XV siècles*, ed. Rosa Maria Dressi and Michel Lauwers, Collection du centre d'études médiévales de Nice 1 (Nice: Centre d'études médiévales, 1997), 271–90.

Intellectual context for the artes praedicandi is also provided by editions and studies of the *ars poeticae* and the *ars dictaminis*. For example:

Camargo, Martin, *Ars dictaminis, ars dictandi* (Turnhout: Brepols, 1991).
—, *Medieval Rhetorics of Prose Composition: Five English Artes dictandi and their Tradition* (Binghamton, NY: Medieval and Renaissance Texts and Studies, 1995).
Kelly, Douglas, *The Arts of Poetry and Prose* (Turnhout: Brepols, 1991).

Notes on the Translation

This translation has benefited immensely from the critique, commentary, and suggestions of Myra L. Uhlfelder (Professor Emerita, Bryn Mawr), who graciously agreed to read it despite many other commitments. Sally A. Wilson particularly wishes to acknowledge the assistance of Kevin Roddy (University of California, Davis), who first introduced her to Ranulph Higden and the *Ars componendi sermones*; of Mark Riley (California State University, Sacramento), who spent untold hours helping her with the translation; and of James Murphy (University of California, Davis), who provided assistance with medieval rhetorical terminology and suggested the translation for publication.

The translation reflects, as closely as contemporary English will permit, the prose style manifest in *The Ars componendi sermones of Ranulph Higden*, ed. Margaret Jennings (Leiden: Brill, 1991). In a very few instances — as in "of preaching" (Latin: *predicacionis*) at the end of the preface — an alternative reading from the Latin edition has been chosen for translation because it accords better with the context; such divergences are indicated in the notes. When sense in English demands the insertion of a word or phrase, the addition appears in square brackets. Square brackets also signal appended scriptural citations; these are generally clear, although it should be remarked that "Eccli." points to Ecclesiasticus (Sirach) and "Eccl." indicates the book entitled Ecclesiastes. Some of these citations, however, differ from Higden's references in the text. Such discrepancies may indicate a faulty memory or the author's use of a Vulgate Bible with chapter and verse enumeration different from what is deemed standard today. One or both of these situations may likewise be responsible for scriptural quotations which contain a non-canonical word. These variants are indicated by the use of plain text, at either end of or within the biblical verse. For consistency, and except on the rare occasions when Higden's discussion dictates an absolutely literal translation, the *New American Catholic (Confraternity) Edition of the Holy Bible* (New York: Benziger Brothers, 1958) is the source for biblical references.

Other bibliographical material has been handled on an *ad hoc* basis. When the name of a text is usually cited in English — like Augustine's *City of God* — that practice continues. When a treatise is either unknown in the vernacular or frequently retains its Latin title — like Augustine's *De doctrina christiana* — no translation has been attempted. A final observation: the *Ars*' vocabulary is periodically affected by the technical jargon of medieval rhetoric, the scholastic terminology employed in the schools, various ecclesiastical usages, and the sometimes confusing fact that medieval Latin relates to classical Latin as American English relates to British English. Since such phenomena change the standard translations of Latin into English, the list below, illustrating the range of signification for selections from Higden's vocabulary, can be useful. The Latin word appears first, followed by its possible meanings.

antiquus (usually in plural): refers to preachers (pre-thirteenth century) who did not use the thematic method in structuring their sermons
circumspeccio: taking appropriate care or exercising appropriate caution
circumstancia: condition, quality, attribute
clavis: literally a key; here, the restatement of a division's parts to clarify them
coloracio: enlivening (a written work) or making a sermon vivid
concordancia: a parallel passage, usually from the Hebrew or Christian Scriptures
condiccio: an existential state, manifested either tangibly or intangibly, like "doctor" or "healer"; also a situation or modality
congruencia: suitability, appropriateness, relevance
dilatacio: embellishment, dilation, or amplification in various ways of sermon material which has been divided and confirmed. A popular treatise by Richard of Thetford recommended eight modes of dilation. Sermon theorists adapted, expanded, or truncated Richard's recommendations; Ranulph Higden discusses ten
impugnans: literally attacking; so, contrary to
enthymema: a form of argumentation in which a premise or the conclusion is unexpressed
manuduccio: something fashioned or adapted to offer guidance
mature: at an appropriate time
modernus (usually in plural): a practitioner of thematic sermon construction
oracio: a prayer; sometimes simply a statement
orthodoxus: literally orthodox; so, correct, sound, reputable
positus: something set out for consideration or proposed
premissio: literally a sending forth; so, something offered
propositum: a theme, a point put forward for commentary or explication

The Art of Composing Sermons

Ranulph Higden

Concerning the Art of Preaching According to Ranulph of Chester[1]

When one is skillfully making sermons, certain general factors must be considered; in particular, the selection of a theme, its introduction, the division of the principal parts and the development or subdivision of the principal divisions, the extension of the subdivision of the members, and their amplification.

As to the selection of the theme, one must realize that this statement should be complete and independent. It should be appropriate or capable of being applied. It ought, I maintain, to be complete at least in meaning, if not always in word and sense. If, however, it is complete in both word and sense, so much the better.

Indeed, I call a statement complete in regard to word and sense when, internally, there is agreement of subject to verb, of case to person, of adjective to substantive; so that whatever pertains to the completion of the statement is obvious to whoever hears it as in, "The Word was made flesh" [John 1.4] or a similar passage. I say that a statement, correct in meaning, is one in which something may be adequately inferred to complete the meaning [as in], "Arise and walk" [Matt. 9.5]. This statement is correct in meaning because it contains the potentiality for adequately completing the meaning. Indeed, a theme ought to be complete in both word and meaning, or at least in meaning.

From this it is clear that a theme ought not to be dependent in such a manner that its completion depends totally on something that is beyond itself. For example, if a preacher were to say, "When Jesus entered the boat" [Matt. 8.23], this statement is certainly incomplete and dependent because it requires extraneous material in order to be understood both in word and sense. Therefore, one should adopt neither this passage nor anything similar as one's theme. In addition, the theme ought to be appropriate or capable of being applied, and I call a theme "appropriate" that literally refers to the matter or the saint about which one intends to preach. So that if one intends to preach about penitence, one may select, "Do penance" [Matt. 4.17]; if about some saint, for example St. John the Baptist, one may select, "There was a man sent from God" [John 1.6]. This is an appropriate theme since it is literally speaking about John. Moreover, I call a theme capable of being applied when it contains something related to what is being preached about; hence, someone may wish to apply to a saint a theme which can be made to suit that purpose. For example, one can appropriately apply to blessed Andrew, suspended on the cross for Christ's love, the passage in Galatians 4, "I am nailed to the cross" [Gal. 2.19]. So much for the selection of the theme.

The next section concerns the introduction of the theme, which should incorporate a fitting exemplum or a suitable proverb or some original saying or something obvious in itself, provided that this section is always short and conducive to devotion. Thirdly, there follows a discussion about the division of the main theme and other matters.

Chapter I: the Preface to this Art

To the surpassing praise of this art, most reputable scholars assert that among the holocausts in both Old and New Testaments, that sacrifice most pleasing to God is accomplished when man, first and principally, offers himself to God through fervent devotion,[2] according to the psalm, "I am bound, O God, by vows to you" [Ps. 55.12]. Secondly and as a result [of this offering] when one brings one's neighbor as near to God as possible through fruitful preaching, as it says at the end of the Apocalypse, "And let everyone who hears say, 'Come'" [Apoc. 22.17], and, in Ecclesiasticus 12, "Each of them he gives precepts about his fellow men" [Eccli. 17.12]. Accordingly, to educate the untutored, those who up to this point were ignorant of the art of preaching, I gathered together excerpts from various authors to be imparted to those sincere of heart. Whatever else is touched upon in my treatise, it is most important to pay attention to the preacher and his sermon.

Three things are necessary in the preacher: correctness of intention, holiness of behavior, and aptitude for public speaking. A sermon should also possess three qualities: relevance of theme, correctness of division, and usefulness of development. Before I discuss these matters, it should be noted that according to some scholars, preaching consists, after the invocation of God's help, of proposing a theme, dividing the theme proposed, subdividing the division, adducing authorities which will support with reasons and examples, interpreting these authorities with a view to increasing the spread of divine worship, enlightening the church militant, and inflaming mankind's love for God. But, according to others, preaching is public persuasion at the proper time and place to promote salvation.[3] Such a description excludes the discourse studied and disputed in the schools since it pertains more to the probing of truth than to preaching. Likewise excluded is private exhortation, and for this reason it is improper to quote John 15, saying that Christ had preached to a Samaritan woman.[4] Likewise barred is the ringing harangue of the warmonger or the quarrelsome debate style of lawsuits.

Moreover, in this art, as in other branches of knowledge, four causes can be discerned: final, material, efficient, and formal.[5] The final cause of preaching ought to include inspiration of the preacher, edification of the listener, and veneration of the creator. The material cause consists in the sermon's having proper words to announce virtues, vices, punishment, and joys. The efficient cause is twofold: God as originator, and the preacher as agent. The formal cause is apparent in the previous description of preaching, and so forth.

Chapter II: [Concerning Correctness of Intention]

Correctness of intention implies that preaching have a proper end. This occurs when one preaches for the glorification of God, for the edification of one's neighbor, and for the teaching of truth — and not for receiving favors as with public administrators, nor for the ostentation of self as with oil vendors,[6] about whom it says in the psalm [Ps. 52.6], "God has scattered the bones of them that please men" (that is those who strain to please), and to the Galatians Paul says, "If I were still trying to please men," that is, turned my attention to pleasing, "I should not be a servant of Christ" [Gal. 1.10]. Even when expedient, the truth should not be concealed, not for love or fear, or hatred or favor, or for an entreaty or bribe, according to the example of Michea the prophet at the end of the third book of Kings who, when the messenger urged him to speak pleasing things to the king, responded, "The Lord liveth; whatsoever the Lord shall say to me, that will I speak" [III Kings 22.13–14]. And thus Chrysostom says, not only is he a liar who openly invents the truth but even more is he a liar who does not freely proclaim the truth when it is necessary for him to pronounce it (XI, quaestio iii, "Nolite"; Extra "quod metus causa," chapter "sacris"[7]). In expressing the truth, one is not always required to have subtlety of speech, because occasionally, plain simplicity teaches more. Accordingly, in Corinthians 2, Paul says, "My speech and my preaching were not in the persuasive words of human wisdom, but in the demonstration of the Spirit" [I Cor. 2.4].

Under this heading as well must be rejected stories lacking in substance or the buffoonery suited to children, for such things are irrelevant to salvation, attracting the ear rather than the soul. About this the Prophet says, your innkeepers mix water with the wine, which is discussed in Distinction 8, "cum multa";[8] it was perhaps of this circumstance that Augustine taught in *De doctrina christiana*, at the end of Book 2, saying that the sons of Israel carried away precious possessions from Egypt, so that they could put them to better use later.[9] In a similar fashion, Jerome, attacking Jovinianus, used the words of the philosophers and the poetry of the pagans.[10]

Chapter III: About Holiness of Behavior

Second, a preacher must exhibit holiness of behavior, for it is spoken in the psalm that to the sinner, "God says: 'Why do you recite my statutes?'" [Ps. 49.16] and so forth and Gregory in a homily[11] says, "Whose life is despised, his preaching is held in contempt" (Distinction XL, "nullus").[12] Thus, Paul chastised his body lest perhaps after preaching to others, he himself should be rejected [see I Cor. 9.27]. When, indeed, the life of a preacher is holy, his sermon will be effective and powerful, as is shown with regard to Blessed Stephen in Acts 2, whom "the Jews were not able to withstand" [Acts 6.10]. Also, in the fourth book of the *Historia ecclesiastica*, it can be read how the Hebrew people were converted to the faith by a certain captive Christian woman.[13] According to Gregory in his *Moralia*, the authority of the spoken word is lost when speech is not supported by works.[14] The same thing is also clear in the second book of his *Pastoral Care*, chapter vii, where it is said that a preacher, like a rooster, should make himself heard more by what he does than by the way he sounds[15] for, as the Philosopher declares in the fourth book of the *Ethics*, when actions and speech disagree, these dissonances hinder the truth.[16]

Chapter IV: Concerning Aptitude for Public Speaking

Third, an aptitude for public speaking is required for anyone preaching, in order that he might proclaim [the Gospel] loudly, fluently, and at an appropriate time. Loudly, in fact, so that it may be heard by everyone; fluently, so that, as it is being delivered, it may be easily understood; at an appropriate time, so that it may be listened to willingly. Such opportuneness, indeed, possesses two aspects: the proper gesture of the body and the well-modulated quality of the voice, about which Valerius Maximus spoke in the eighth book of the *Gesta memorabilia*. Citing the example of the philosopher Hortensius, [he said] it was uncertain if a large crowd came to watch Hortensius' graceful gestures or to hear what he had to say.[17]

Since the preacher assumes the role of an orator, the nature of his movement and delivery has a great influence on the mind of the listener. Let him temper his gesture in order that, as the material about which he is preaching varies, so his movement and delivery also should be varied. Hugh of St. Victor deals with this in his *On Noviceship*, saying: one should speak with words alone, without excessively displaying one's arms or hands as flatterers do, or by moving one's head, exaggerating one's facial expression, and averting one's eyes as hypocrites do.[18] Augustine spoke about this matter in his *De doctrina christiana*: serious things, he said, must be discussed in an appropriate manner;[19] for example, when wickedness is preached against, it should be done stingingly and with disgust, as in the psalm, "Falsehood I hate" [Ps. 118.163] and so forth. Likewise, Seneca, in Epistle 184: "Against vices, I want something to be said harshly; against dangers, courageously; against fate, haughtily; against ambition, critically; against extravagance, reproachfully."[20] Thus Seneca's words.

In addition, when virtue is preached about, let the sermon be more restrained as if beseeching the hearer to embrace virtues, as in Romans 11, "I exhort you … to present your bodies as a living sacrifice" [Rom. 12.1]. When punishments are preached about, let the vocabulary and gesture be more frightening; for example, in Luke 3, John the Baptist says, "Brood of vipers, who has shown you how to flee?" [Luke 3.7]. When rewards are preached about, let word and gesture be more uplifting and more pious, as in Colossians 3, "Mind the things that are above" [Col. 3.2].

Moreover, to an aptitude for public speaking should be added an appropriate time for speaking, according to Ecclesiastes 8, "There is a time and a judgment for everything" [Eccl. 8.6]. Indeed, a preacher should not speak on all occasions or everywhere, but at a suitable time and place. For if the heavens were always raining, the earth would not germinate. Whence Bede said, commenting on Luke: not every occasion is conducive to learning.[21]

Chapter V: About Appropriate Care in Speaking

In this endeavor, appropriate care in speaking requires that one form one's sermon according to the capacity of one's listeners, as Gregory teaches in *On Ezechiel*, Book I, homily 41[22] and in the *Moralia* 24, stating that a teacher should consider what he says, to whom he says it, how he says it, and how much is stated.[23] Four things necessary to this art are indicated here: the meaning of the words to be spoken, the "what he says"; the nature of the listeners, the "to whom he says it"; the manner of speaking, the "how it is said"; the duration of the whole speech, the "how much is said."

Concerning the first of these requisites, that is, the material spoken about, let the content of what is said be considered under four headings: cursing vices, recommending virtues, threatening punishments, and encouraging rewards. The entire Sacred Scripture directs itself to enunciating these things according to Timothy 3, "All scripture is inspired by God and useful for teaching, for reproving, for correcting, for instructing" [II Tim. 3.16]. Indeed, for teaching the glory to be striven for, [this verse] in Romans 5, "Whatever things have been written, have been written for our instruction" [Rom. 15.4]. Likewise, for reproving those committing crimes, [this verse] in Ecclesiastes 20, "The sayings of the wise are like goads" [Eccl. 12.11]. Again, for correcting those who do not fear punishment, [this verse] in Jeremias 23, "Are not my words as a fire ... and as a hammer that breaketh the rock in pieces?" [Jer. 23.29]. Also, for instructing those who neglect virtue, it says thus in Daniel 12: "They that instruct many to justice [shall shine] as stars for all eternity" [Dan. 12.3].

Concerning the second of those requisites, which is the nature of the listeners, let the preacher consider carefully "to whom" he speaks because at some times he must talk to different types of people, at other times to similar types of people who are, nevertheless, struggling with a variety of vices or who are in diverse situations. Gregory proposes an example in his *Moralia* 14, of the physician who looks carefully at the wound before he bandages it and also of the farmer who studies the nature of the land before he sows it.[24] With the preacher in mind, it is said in Job 38, "[Who] gives the cock its understanding" [Job 38.36]; hence Gregory says in *Moralia* 30: understanding has been allotted to the cock just as the power of discretion is granted to the preacher, so that he will know clearly what, when, and whom he is teaching.[25] For, not one and the same exhortation is suitable to all people because not all have the same character, as it says in the third book of the *Pastoral Care*: a soft whistle calms horses but stirs up whelps.[26] And, as Gregory says at the end of this book:[27] however laborious it is to instruct each individual properly, it is more laborious to admonish at the same time and in the same words diverse listeners who are afflicted with different passions, so as to insure that humility is preached to the proud while the faintheartedness of the timid is not increased. Moreover, in a related circumstance, it is more difficult to preach to one and the same man who is a slave to opposing vices in such a manner as to cure one vice without increasing the others, although it is better to suppress that vice which stands out as more dangerous, even though it is not possible to hold that one in check without an increase in a lesser vice.

Concerning the third of these requisites, that is, the manner of speaking, let the preacher consider how he makes his case, so that he is not so succinct and clipped in speaking that he may be found elliptical, nor so diffuse that he may be considered tedious, nor so obscure that he might not be understood, nor so aggressive that he might be deemed spiteful, nor so ostentatious that he might be seduced by pride, nor so overscrupulous that his sermon might be thought insignificant.

Concerning the fourth of these requisites, that is, the duration of the whole sermon, let the preacher consider how much is to be said since profound things must be communicated to the wise and common things to the simple. About the first of these, it says in Corinthians 2, "Wisdom ... we speak among those who are mature" [I Cor. 2.6]; concerning the second, Corinthians 4 has, "I fed you with milk, not with solid food, for you were not yet ready for it" [I Cor. 3.2], according to the example of Christ who taught the crowds on the flat land and in the countryside; however, He instructed his disciples on the mountain. Whence He said in Luke, "To you it is given to know the mystery of the kingdom of God" [Luke 8.10], but to the uneducated and weak, He said in John 16: "Many things I have yet to say to you, but you cannot bear them now" [John 16.12]. And Gregory, at the end of the second book of the *Pastoral Care,* [says] a preacher should be careful that he does not stretch the mind of the listener beyond his capacity, lest in pulling too hard, he break the cords of the mind.[28] For this reason Moses veiled his face in front of the people, because he did not want to reveal the secrets of the law to the untutored.[29] Therefore, in Job 16 it is said that "he who binds up" water "in the clouds,"[30] constricts the knowledge of doctrine in those preaching so that [the unlearned] may be nourished not by a cloudburst of wisdom but by its measured dripping down.

Chapter VI: Concerning the Suitability of the Theme

Now, about those things which affect the sermon itself: it should be noted that a suitable theme must not be obscure but plainly impart understanding; second, that it be relevant to the matter being addressed; third, that it be from a biblical text; fourth, that it be divisible into not more than three parts; fifth, that it allow for real and verbal concordance; sixth, that from this theme the antetheme or protheme (which is the same thing) can be derived.

With regard to the first of these [requisites], one must note that some themes are complete, others incomplete; some general, others particular; some accommodated, others misconstrued. A theme is complete when, having been correctly constructed, it contains the predicate as well as the subject of the verb, as here, "Christ died for us" [Rom. 5.9]. A theme is incomplete when one must supply a subject or a predicate;

so, if one says, "died for all" [II Cor. 5.15], the subject "Christ" is implied. Likewise, if speaking about some virgin, one were to say, "The virgin daughter of Syon" [IV Kings 19.21], the meaning seems uncertain and incomplete because the verb is left out. A theme is general when it is able to be used on any feast day; for instance, "Serve ye the Lord with fear" [Ps. 2.11] and this, The Lord "guided [the just] in direct ways" [Wis. 10.10]. A theme is particular when it fits the specific occasion of the sermon, as is shown in the next chapter. A theme is accommodated when it speaks literally about one thing but is adapted to another through a mystical signification, as this from Kings 28, "Jonathan stripped himself of his coat" [I Kings 18.4]. Although this passage literally speaks about Jonathan, the son of Saul, allegorically it is able to be said of Saint Bartholomew. A theme is misconstrued when that which literally is said of some opprobrious person is applied to some holy person, as in Kings 18, "I saw Absolom hanging upon an oak" [II Kings 18.10]. If this were used to comment upon Christ or Saint Andrew, it would be especially faulty because Sacred Scripture is well supplied with relevant themes which can be selected.

Chapter VII: Let the Theme relate to the Proposed Subject Matter

In order that the suitability of the theme be more fully demonstrated, it must first be remarked that there are three different categories of sermons according to the occasion on which they are preached: the Sunday sermon, the feast-day sermon, and the sermon for different circumstances of people[31] or for diverse affairs like visitations, elections, synods, and processions.[32] Wherefore, he who must preach about the Advent season should choose something like, "The desired shall come" [Ag. 2.8]; about the Nativity of the Lord, "Grace ... appeared" [Tit. 2.11] or "A light has arisen" [Matt. 4.16]; during Lent, "Do penance" [Matt. 4.17]; at Easter, "The Lord has risen indeed" [Luke 24.34], and so in other times. Likewise, if one must preach about a saint, he should look at what is most celebrated and praiseworthy about that saint, and from this he should set forth his theme. For example, of Blessed Andrew, since he hung on a cross preaching for a long time, to him is able to be applied that text in Galatians 4, "I am nailed to the Cross" [Gal. 2.19]. Similarly, Blessed Nicholas, because he is especially noteworthy for his compassionate works, can have applied to him this passage from Job, "From my infancy, mercy grew with me" [Job 31.18] and of [blessed] Martin, "[He] hath covered the naked with a garment" [Ezech. 18.7 and 16]. Similarly, in sermons for affairs like elections, let one say, "Choose the best" [IV Kings 10.3]; for synods, "Be ye clean, you that carry the vessels of the Lord" [Is. 52.11]; for visitations, [a verse] in Ezechiel 33, "The shepherd visiteth his flock" [Ezech. 34.12]; in processions and to implore peace, "Pray ye for the things that are for peace" [see Ps. 121.6];

against the plague,[33] "O Lord, save us, we perish" [Matt. 8.25]; for funerals, "Our friend sleeps" [John 11.11].

Chapter VIII: Let the Theme be from the Bible

It is right and indeed necessary on every occasion to select a theme from the Bible, provided that the theme be neither apocryphal nor accommodated; for example, if one says on the Feast of the Trinity, "He saw three and worshipped one," this is not permitted because it is not a biblical text.[34] Also, on the Feast of the Annunciation of the Lord or the Visitation, it is wrong to propose, "Go into the garden with me" because the correct reading is, "I went into my garden."[35] Likewise, if it is said about some saint, "My foot has always walked in" the steps of God [Job 23.11], this is also not permitted because the correct reading is "his steps." Nor is it allowed at any time to substitute a word in one verse for that in another, so if one simply were to state, "Say among the peoples that the Lord reigns from a tree," this would not be acceptable because the Vulgate reading is, "Say among the nations that the Lord reigns" [Ps. 95.10]. Of course, one might wonder why the previous version is not acceptable, for its truth is obvious in the writing of Blessed Ambrose: "These things are fulfilled which David sings in a song of faith, telling the nations that God reigns from a tree."[36]

As I was saying, there are two reasons why themes from unknown sources are not acceptable. The first is because proposing such obscure passages seems to indicate that the preacher is grasping for praise, as if he himself knows those things which are unknown to others. The second reason is because, if this were permitted, then heretics would be able to create their own themes and impose a metaphorical meaning, and thus bring about error.[37] For this reason it seems Christ himself used that theme which his herald John the Baptist had chosen beforehand — that is, "Do penance!"

Nevertheless, one can omit certain unnecessary words in a theme, for instance conjunctions and adverbs. Thus, if we say, "Let us lay aside the works of darkness" [Rom. 13.12], here the word "therefore" is omitted without invalidating the theme. Likewise, even when the correct text is actually, "Now, indeed, our salvation is nearer" [Rom. 13.11], one can say, "Now our salvation is nearer"; and when the correct text is, "And he walks not in the way of sinners" [Ps. 1.1], one can omit the linking word "and" since, by this omission, the signification is more comprehensive. But, in the middle of a theme, such a linking word cannot be eliminated; thus, when the correct biblical verse is, "Heal me, O Lord, and I shall be healed" [Jer. 17.14], one cannot say about the Magdalene: "Heal me, O Lord, I shall be healed."[38] Also, neither in the beginning nor in the end can other conjunctions that create conditional sentences be omitted, although a preceding interjection can be left out as long as the sentence remains complete. Thus, in exhorting to war, one can say, "I will comfort myself over my adversaries" [Is. 1.24], although the correct biblical verse is, "Ah, I will comfort myself" and so forth.

Certainly, other significant parts cannot be left out if by this omission the meaning is changed. For example, if on Pentecost, the theme "The spirit of wisdom came" were selected, this is not acceptable because the correct text is, "The spirit of wisdom came to me" [Wis. 7.7]. However, it is all right to eliminate the word "wisdom," thus saying, "The spirit came to me." Similarly, it is not permissible to change the tense of a verb, so when the biblical verse is, "He shall go up that shall open the way before them" [Mi. 2.13], it cannot be said on the Ascension: "He goes up, opening the way before them."

In addition, not only is a biblical text altered through the omission of a word, it is also corrupted as, for example, if in place of, "How [will you believe] if I speak to you?" [John 3.12] is said simplistically, "If I speak to you of heavenly things, you will believe." For Christ made this statement interrogatively and negatively, as if he were saying, "You will not believe." If it is manipulated into implying the opposite, this is a corruption.

The same corruption occurs when a theme is applied to a subject inappropriate to it. For example, if on Easter is said, "Trypho arose," [this is a corruption] since Trypho was very evil.[39] Likewise, [it is unacceptable] to substitute, using the same word, one meaning for another; for example, if on Palm Sunday, the verse used is, "I know, O Lord, that your ordinances are equitable" [Ps. 118.75] and then the word *equitable* (*equitas*) is related to Christ's riding on the ass (*equitacione Christi*). A related corruption: if speaking about Saint Edmund the King, "The wicked have bent their bows" [Ps. 10.3] were selected, and in this theme's development, an authority were cited for *have bent* (*intenderunt*)[40], like "Harken to my voice" [Ps. 140.1] or "O Lord, make haste to help me" [Ps. 69.1], which creates a different signification. Similarly, a corruption occurs when an incomplete preceding clause is added to a subsequent clause; for example, if one were to say to penitents, "Be repentant [Ps. 4.5]; offer up the sacrifice of justice" [Ps. 4.6].

Nevertheless, some truncation, rearrangement, and substitution of meaning is allowed, as long as it is not excessive and obvious. Thus, if on the first Sunday of Lent is said, "You receive the grace of God," the text is acceptably altered in that what the Apostle said negatively is stated positively. The Apostle's text is actually, "[We entreat] you not to receive the grace of God in vain" [II Cor. 6.1] and so forth, wherein two things are stated, that is, "They receive grace" and "so that they do not receive it in vain." Similarly, if on Easter Sunday, it were said, "[Her husband] rose and opened the door" [Jud. 19.27]. In relating this passage literally to Christ, great incongruity occurs since the Book of Judges actually is speaking of a Levite who divorced his wife.

Of course, a moral reading can sometimes be substituted for the literal signification. If it is said about some martyr, "He struck the rock," and "waters gushed forth" [Ps. 77.20], in a literal sense, this refers to the striking of a good man; in a moral sense, the smiting of a bad man.

Chapter IX: Let the Theme be Adequately Divided

Above all, one must be sure that the theme selected should be such that enough divisions can be made. This is quite clear when the theme contains three meaningful words, such as, "Your king comes" [Matt. 21.5]. There are, however, some words with which a division is not able and ought not to be made, like prepositions, conjunctions, and the word *is* when it is followed by a predicate adjective or when it is used as an auxiliary verb. So if the theme were, "The just man is delivered from trouble" [Prov. 11.8], no division should be made using the words *is* (*est*) or *from* (*de*). But, when the word *is* is self-contained and its action expresses its own substance as here, "I AM sent me to you" [Ex. 3.14] or here, "But you are the same" [Ps. 101.28], then the division can fall on the word *are* (*es*), since thus is signified identity, existence, and oneness of nature.

Whatever their length, verses able to be divided into two or three parts are acceptable as themes; for example, on the birth of Our Lord or on the Annunciation, this theme is proposed, "God sent his son, born of a woman, born under the Law that [he might redeem] those who" [Gal. 4.4–5] and so forth; even though there are seventeen words in that text, it is still able to be divided into three parts. Thus, three things are said: indicated here is how the healer's assistance is abundantly lavished, in the words, "He sent his son"; secondly, how humility, powerfully displayed, heals because the Son was "born of a woman, born under the law"; thirdly, how helpfulness, fruitfully expended, is channeled in many directions, where it reads "that he might redeem those who were under the Law." These partitioned sections admit division into parts; for example, in *God* (*Deus*) simplicity shines forth, in *sent* (*misit*) expenditure, in *son* (*filius*) abundance, and so for the other members. Nothing should be lacking and thus these three can be confirmed by three authorities or by one in which verbally there are the three words, *God*, *sent*, and *son*; hence, great profundity may meaningfully be communicated. But because it is difficult to find such authorities, generally themes containing these many words are not subsumed into a single division.

Sometimes it happens that the theme contains only two words but, as they can be fashioned into three parts, a threefold division is thus made. For example, a theme about Saint Nicholas, "The child grew" [Gen. 21.8], is able to be developed thus: Nicholas is praised for his state of purity in *child*, for his increase in worthiness in *grew*, and in both for the reward of fruitfulness in "The child grew." At this point it is required that the third member be given authority consonant to that of the other divisions by a text which contains those two words, *grew* and *child*.

Nevertheless, modern usage rejects lengthy themes and more than three divisions, unless, when speaking in the vernacular to the people, a concise text from the Gospel is chosen and, in tracking down its meaning, the Gospel is explained phrase by phrase, without any subdivision. Concerning this practice, Brother James of Genoa observes in his *Collaciones suis dominicalibus quadragesimalibus*,[41] that this is useful for common folk. There is another practice which is similar to this, as in the theme about the apostles, "Are there not twelve hours?"[42] Immediately, it is possible to elaborate thus: the first hour of the day can be called "Peter" for a variety of reasons, and so on for the other apostles. Likewise, a theme with a conjunction can be divided into two equal sections as in, "Let us [therefore] lay aside the works of darkness and put on the armor of light" [Rom. 13.12], wherein two things are mentioned that the Apostle invites us to do: the abandoning of sins and the putting on of virtues. The theme can be of one word if it permits expansion so as to imply more things, especially if the words are exhortations like *Understand!*, *Consider!*, *Go!*, *Preach!*, *Walk!*. Otherwise, consult the above discussion if the word does not fully express the meaning, as could occur on the Purification, if the theme "Light" were chosen.

Chapter X: Let the Theme allow for Parallel Passages

It is necessary in any theme that its meaningful and significant components allow for authorities on which verbal and actual parallels can easily be brought to bear. Otherwise, he will be a foolish preacher who too often limits himself to barren words, especially since abundant material from Sacred Scripture is available. Although earlier preachers did not observe this [precept], let there, nevertheless, be verbal agreement among the principal divisions as well as among the secondary divisions. This is not possible in a theme of one word like *Walk!*, yet it can be stated that threefold is the path: flat, straight, and clear. About the straight path of God's commands, it says in Matthew, "Make straight your paths, the footsteps of God" [see Matt. 3.3 and Is. 40.3]. Certainly, this is the path spoken of in Isaias, "[This is the way,] walk ye in it; [and] go not aside neither to the right hand nor to the left" [Is. 30.21]. Because this statement is made about the path, there is no verbal concordance with *Walk!*, but since the division is constructed with one authority containing the word *walk*, that ought to be enough.

If someone is preaching in English, *to go* can be used instead of *to walk*, since in English the words are interchangeable. For example, if it is said, first one must walk

of Oxford, but the Parisian practice is this:[54] we see by experience that if something is fumigated with red sulfur, it smells and loses color; but if it is fumigated with incense, it regains its color. In the moral sense, the sulfurous smoke is sin, as in the psalm, "He rains upon the wicked fiery coals and brimstone" [Ps. 10.7] and so forth. The incensed smoke is prayer, whose sound ascends straight up, not obliquely, as in the psalm: "May my prayer come like incense before you" [Ps. 140.2].

Also, the invocation can be set up from the beginning, even though it does not stem from the theme itself. Thus, if it is said: although one has sight as long as the visible object is present, yet he cannot see without light; so the soul, even though capable of understanding, profits nothing without mediating grace, as is stated in John 15, "Without me, you can do nothing" [John 15.5]. Therefore, let us ask for grace from the outset.

Chapter XIII: About Winning over the Audience

It is expedient for the preacher, as long as this is inoffensive to God, that from the start he render his audience willing and attentive listeners and concerned about following the argument. This can be done in many ways. In the first one, let something unusual, subtle, and curious be proposed — possibly [the narrative] of some authentic miracle — which is able to be applied to the topic and attract the audience. For example, if the theme were, "A spring rose out of the earth" [Gen. 2.6], reference to a certain fountain in Cicilia which Gerald of Wales talks about in his *Topographia hibernie* can be made: whenever anyone dressed in a red gown approached this fountain, immediately water was released from it; however, the fountain remained undisturbed in the face of anyone clothed otherwise.[55] That fountain is Christ, about whom it is said in Ecclesiasticus, "The word of God on high is a fountain of wisdom" [Eccli. 1.5]. One approaching it in a red gown, that is Christ during his passion, draws forth the living waters of grace.[56] Indeed, by the flowing blood of Christ, "the earth quaked and the rocks were rent" [Matt. 27.51]. Unless they are harder than rocks, how much more ought your hearts be moved and split open at the call of the word of God.[57]

This method is also effective when the cause of some obscure saying is pointed out. So, if why the eye is not a fixed color is discussed, the answer is because, if it were, it would perceive only one hue — the color of the eye itself — and there ought to be as many perceptions as colors.[58] This saying can be applied to sinners, especially the avaricious and deceitful who, in that they are fixed in opposition, do not perceive the operation of God's word.

Another method is to frighten the congregation from the outset with some terrible story or exemplum, as James of Vitry narrates about someone who, never willing to hear the word of God, was, after his death, brought to the church for burial. When the priest was to begin the prayers for the dead, the figure on the crucifix — the crucifix stood between the nave of the church and the choir — ripped his palms away from the nails and covered his ears, lest he hear the prayer made for the dead one who, while alive, never wanted to hear the word of God crucified. In the same situation preachers utilize other comparable stories, in one of which Christ, appearing to the deceased, held blood from his side in his palm and proceeded to throw it into the face of this hardened sinner saying: "This blood which your hardened heart despised will bear witness against you on the Day of Judgment." It was discovered later that the blood, thrown at him in this way, was not able to be removed by any process but remained on the body even after it had been buried.[59]

Another method is to show how those who willingly hear the word of God are eligible for many rewards.

Chapter XIV: Concerning the Introduction of the Theme

According to the method of the moderns, after the prayer has been made, the theme is to be taken up again. It should be noted from what book it was taken and even the chapter, just as was done initially. Henceforth, it is not generally required to indicate more than the chapter, unless a professor of theology wishes to cite all things carefully; [on the other hand,] that which is from a common source should not be too briefly identified, as in [the phrase], "the Scripture says." The book from which the authority was selected should be mentioned at all times.

At last, the theme having been recapitulated, the introduction is able to be made in many ways: through scripture, through argument, through adapting an example, through a simile from nature, through a vernacular saying. For example, in the first of these ways, let the theme be, "A marriage took place at Cana of Galilee" [John 2.1]. According to Augustine,[60] the words of Sacred Scripture have a fourfold meaning: historical, tropological, allegorical, and anagogical, and according to this structure these words of John the Evangelist can be understood literally to refer to a wedding; according to the allegorical sense to the marriage of Christ and our nature in the womb of the Virgin; according to the tropological, that is, the moral sense, to the union of the human soul with Christ through grace; according to the anagogical sense, the wedding of our soul to Christ in Paradise is understood. And then, let the development be made according to the sense which, among all, is most applicable. Let this same method be used in the themes which have many meanings.

Likewise, on the Lord's Annunciation, the theme [might be], "The young man will dwell with the virgin" [Is. 62.5]. This can be introduced through Sacred Scripture.

In the Law [Torah] it was taught that the high priest might not take as his wife either a divorcee or a harlot, but only a virgin from his tribe.[61] But since about the Son of God it says, "You are a priest forever" [Ps. 109.4] and so forth, he ought to be associated with a virgin. Although this was mystically authenticated about Christ and his Church according to the Apostle in Corinthians, "I betrothed you to one spouse [that I might present you] a chaste virgin" (II Cor. 11.2] and so forth, this was literally authenticated about Christ and the glorious Virgin with whom he began today to dwell as his mother, wife, and sister, as Isaias foresaw saying, "The young man will dwell with the virgin."

Likewise, this same theme is introduced from the writing of the saints[62] thus: nothing [in the same way] so causes discord among us as the bonds of matrimony. But since our nature could not bear the divine disfavor which it incurs through sin, it was necessary that some virgin bride be provided for Christ by whose marriage this disfavor might be removed and we might more confidently be able to approach Christ as a son-in-law, or even as a man from our own family, as if a son of our sister, as Augustine says in book four of the *Confessions*: our very Life came down to earth and, bearing our death, He destroyed it and thundering He called us to return to Him in that secret place from which he came forth to us, that is, the virgin's womb, where our nature — mortal flesh — married him lest it forever be mortal.[63] Isaiah foresaw this marriage when he said, "The young man will dwell with the virgin."

Again this same theme is introduced through philosophic or poetic writing, as Seneca says in a certain letter to Lucillius: "Do you wonder whether men come to God or God to men?"[64] Indeed, it is a greater thing that he comes to men, but since he comes to men, in no one [does he come] more than in Him whose son He calls Himself when He says, "The Son of Man came to seek and to save what was lost" [Luke 19.10]. Truly, He alone is the son of man because He is the son only of a Mother. Moreover, "son of men" is not said because He did not have a human being for His father as everyone else does, exactly as Isaias foresaw when he said, "Behold a virgin shall conceive" [Is. 7.14]. In regard to the virgin, the verse can be understood poetically: a virgin very becoming, from the seed and offspring of King David.[65] In a certain homily on Advent, Augustine recites a specific verse from Virgil: "Now the virgin returns, the Saturnian kingdoms return; now the new offspring is sent down from the lofty heavens."[66] For, on that day, the offspring of heaven was sent down into the womb of the Virgin, and then that from Isaiah was fulfilled, ["The young man] will dwell" and so forth.

Again, the introduction is able to be made through an argument or proof, for there are as many modes of argument as there are modes of introduction: namely, by induction, or by example, or by syllogism, or by enthymeme. And first by induction thus: let the theme be, "For those who love God, all things work together unto good"

[Rom. 8.28]. It may be said here that whatever is in this world is either favorable or adverse; but if anyone loves God, the favorable things of the world cause in him fear of the present life, while the adverse ones cause love for the next life. Therefore, "For those who love God, all things work together unto good."

Likewise, syllogistically thus: all things that come from correct reasoning, according to proper desire and thinking, work together toward their good; but for lovers of God, all things occur according to the thinking of correct reason and proper desire; and therefore, "For those who love God," and so forth. Again, a proof by enthymeme would work this way: to those hating God, all things work together unto evil; therefore, "For those who love God," and so forth. In this kind of introduction, if there be anything uncertain in the theme, it is necessary to make it credible and conjoin the demonstration with the theme. In these methods of argument, the Parisians introduce particulars through authorities; for example, as a figure of the text cited above ("Whatever is in the world is either favorable or adverse"), one can say, the Lord divided all time into a "day" of prosperity and a "night" of adversity.[66]

In addition, a theme is introduced by adapting an example thus: if the theme were the same as that above, "The young man will dwell with the virgin," it might be developed in this way: when a monstrous and dangerous war is waged between two kingdoms, peace cannot be established in any stronger way than to have the son of one king marry the daughter of the other.[67] In like manner, after the first sin, there was a monstrous war between the heavenly and earthly kingdoms which could not be settled until the son of heaven joined a daughter of earth to himself by the pact of marriage. The union has been celebrated today, but many years earlier it was announced by the prophet when he said, "The young man will dwell" and so forth.

Again, the theme is introduced, as follows, by a similitude from nature. The strongest animals — the elephant and the unicorn — are captured in this manner: the elephant becomes mild through the song of a virgin and the unicorn grows tame on the lap of a virgin;[68] so also, having been shown the breasts of a virgin, does the most powerful Son of God, as is said in Luke, "Blessed is the womb that bore thee and the breasts that nursed thee" [Luke 11.27]. [The most powerful Son of God] was softened by the song of a virgin when she sang "Behold the handmaid of the Lord" [Luke 1.38]. Similar to the ferocious unicorn is God's Son who destroyed those men and angels who opposed him and aspired to what was beyond them; but he became mild like the unicorn when he grew [the body for] his sacrifice in the lap of the virgin, thereby fulfilling Isaias, "The young man will dwell with the virgin."

Likewise, an introduction [can be made] through an example drawn from the arts. Here we see that a physician, when approaching a sick person, first induces in him the spirit of recovery so that the patient, believing everything he takes will help him, may be more easily cured. But our physician is God and we too are ill;[69] if therefore we show devotion to and confidence in God, all things will assist us to heal our disease, which is sin. And so it is that [the text] says, "For them who love God" and so forth.

Again, an introduction [can be made] through an example from history, as Valerius Maximus did in *De gestis memoralibus*, telling about two good friends, one of whom was willing to die for the other on an appointed day according to the order of the tyrant [Dionysius].[70] Dionysius was so astonished at the steadfastness of the friendship that he rescinded the penalty and joined their fellowship. Behold how faithful friendship achieved a commutation of the death sentence, softened the tyrant, gave life, revealed the nature of fidelity. So, to them that love one another, all things work together unto good, but much more, "[For them who love] God all things work together unto good."

Likewise, an introduction can be made through a commonplace proverb. Let the theme be, "The young man will dwell with the virgin," which can be explicated in four statements: for "young man": "like seeks like,"[71] and every being approves of what is similar to it; since there is great likeness between a young man and a virgin, this can be pointed to immediately in "will dwell." Again, if the theme were, "Keep yourselves holy, because I am holy" [Lev. 11.44], it is said in common parlance, "As the master, so the household";[72] hence for us who ought to be of the household of God, it is right that we conform to his precepts to which we are exhorted in these words, "Keep yourselves holy."

The preceding introductory formats are valid for themes of [at least] two words, as shown above. In themes of one word, it is not appropriate to use all these methods. In reference thereto, modern preachers oppose making a prolix introduction, as Brother Guy did in his sermons[72a]: "For it is a foolish thing to make a long prologue and to be short in the story itself" [II Mac. 2.33]. But if the theme is of one word, it can be introduced by an authority as long as three parts can be developed from that authority which suit the theme and the feast day. For example, let the theme be "Understand!" Here it can be said, as Plato did in the *Timaeus*: God is supreme; envy is far removed from the supreme.[73] Consequently, according to the capacity of their nature, God wished all things to be capable of goodness; so that just as He Himself is good, so all things were to be good. And as He had understanding, so other things were to possess understanding, according to the capacity of their nature. Hence, there is something in the nature of things which knows all by its essence and that is God alone. There is also something which knows all, but partly by its species, partly by its essence, and this is an angel. Therefore, not only are there many modes of knowing, there are many intellectual natures, so many that Aristotle seems to imagine an "ensouled heaven."[74] In the empyrean, God Himself resides as emperor, discerning and governing. In the lower heaven, and occasionally in the ether in the middle, the angel as helper serves; in the lower world, as in a suburb, mankind, like a stranger, struggles to be obedient. In these circumstances, the holy man always submits to the supreme power because through true teaching he is conformed to the divine intellect, through purity of life he is made equal to the angelic intellect, and through sharpness of suffering he is raised up in a certain way above human understanding. Hence, concerning him, one can truly perceive that he shone forth in the gift of teaching, that he flourished through the purity of his life, that he became pre-eminent by victory in battle.[75] Thus in these three parts [the preacher] has effectively fleshed out what was implied in that one word, "Understand!"

Likewise, here is another method of explication. Let the theme be "Walk!" It is necessary in this life that each person either go forward or backward because according to Bernard, it is almost impossible for someone to remain on the same level of goodness for a long time.[76] Since it is dangerous to go backward but profitable to go forward, the Lord says, "Every place your feet tread shall be [yours, therefore] 'walk!'"

Chapter XV: Concerning the Division of the Theme

In dividing, one must form the divisions according to the significance of the words, lest the same word, or a word virtually the same, or a word inappropriate or contrary be both the divider and the divided. An example: if the theme were, "A wise servant is favored by the king" [Prov. 14.35], [and the preacher said that] these three things relate to that holy man: the perfection of wisdom because of "wise," the humility of serving because of "servant," and the favor of the divine because of "is favored." This division would be faulty in every point because of the excessive similarity between the words "wise" and "wisdom," "servant" and "serving," "is favored" and "favor." However, if the same text is explicated using other words, the division would not be faulty. For example, if it could be stated in these words that three things are discussed here: the perfection of reason in "wise," the submission of spirit in "servant," the pleasure of the divine being in "is favored."

It is similarly faulty if in the theme, "The young man will dwell with the virgin" [Is. 62.5], it should be stated that these three things are signaled: the familial dwelling of the son of God because of "will dwell"; second, the unique union with God because of "young man";[77] and third, the contemporaneous condition of girlhood and motherhood because of "with the virgin." Here there is a threefold deficiency because in the first division is put a word which is too closely related to one within the theme, that is, "will dwell"; in the second division, an inappropriate usage occurs because "union" does not signify "young man"; and in the third, a virtually synonymous noun appears because "girl" and "virgin" mean the same thing.

Therefore, a division ought to be fashioned with other descriptive terms, especially those that are oriented to and appropriate for the words which express the members of the division. For example, "to dwell" is to stay for some length of time in a certain place; the proper modality for youth is beauty or joy, because youth is joyous by nature just as an old man is sad and angry;[78] the status of the virgin is purity of mind and body. Likewise, the situation set forth in the division ought to be obvious in the authority by which that member of the division is confirmed as, for example, the rest or stay which is associated with "dwelling" is clear in this authority, "Shall he sojourn in your tent? Shall he dwell?" [Ps. 14.1] and so forth. Similarly, the condition of youth, which is joy, is obvious in this authority, "I will go in to the altar of God, the God of my gladness and joy" [Ps. 42.4]. The status of the virgin, which is purity, is reflected in this authority, "The virgin thinks about the things" of God "that she may be holy in body and spirit" [I Cor. 7.34]. Consequently, the theme is able to be divided in this manner: in the first part, here we are delighted by the long and pleasant rest coming to us from God as is implied in "will dwell," whence is said in the psalm, "Shall he sojourn in your tent? Shall he dwell on your holy mountain?" In the second part, we are gladdened by the beautiful and smiling face of the newborn as is implied in "young man," whence is said in the psalm, "I will go in to the altar of God" and so forth. In the third part, we marvel at the glorious and spotless quality of the one giving birth as is implied in "with the virgin," whence in Corinthians, "The virgin thinks about the things of God" and so forth.

Also it must be noted here that in order to make parallel citations, agreement must be apparent not only with reference to the original word but also with reference to that derived from the original, as *rejoicing* derives from *joy*, and *youthfulness* from *youth*;[79] but if the meanings of the words are not in accord with the divisions, then one must resort to the associated attributes of the words, such as case, number, gender, and even the qualities of the theme, which are "who," "what," "where," "by what means," "why," "how," "when." For example, let the theme about the Nativity be, "I bring you good news of great joy which shall be to all the people, for [today] in the town of David a Savior has been born" [Luke 2.10]. Here might be considered "who" because of "angel," "what" because of "joy," "where" because of "in the town of David," "to whom" because of "to you."

Again, in dividing, it must be understood that one word cannot be placed in front of others, as when the initial division is developed around the second word of the theme rather than the first unless, by this, the order of arrangement, the order of action, or the order of narration is tightened up. An example occurs in this theme, "A wise servant is favored by the king," where the order [of action] is thus: to the extent that the understanding of doing good precedes, appropriate behavior follows, and from these a pleasing reward results. And so, here the division falls first on the word *wise*; second, on the word *servant*, third on *is favored*. Likewise, insofar as this purity of life proximately leads to wisdom and grace, thus, according to the order of arrangement, the division is placed first on the innocence of life, that is on the word *servant*, second on the accompanying wisdom, so on *wise*, and third on pleasing compliance, so on *is favored*. Furthermore, according to the order of narration, the division can be set up according to Augustine's [dictum that] grace comes before all good works, but that the will might efficaciously desire good results from both grace and will.[80] According to the saints, the perfection of knowledge accompanies that order which the psalmist expresses saying, "Teach me goodness," namely of preceding grace, "and discipline," namely of obedient humility, "and "knowledge" [Ps. 118.66], namely of perfect truth.

Similarly, it must be remembered in dividing that when a theme is wholly oriented toward narrating, or describing, or threatening, or disdaining, or promising, or agreeing, or searching, or terrifying, or rebuking, the nature of the words ought to be respected so that if we are enticing our listeners, it might not be said that we are rebuking or vice versa, because this would be ridiculous. For example, the text of Matthew, "Why do you stand here all day idle?" [Matt 20.6] is not to be developed so that it might affirm: here we are exhorted to work. This is stated inappropriately even though it can be said. Indeed, [the theme] must be articulated correctly so that its dominant sense is explicated; for example, here Christ rebukes the lazy and those neglecting work, in part because of their nature when He says, "Why do you stand?" — that is, you who are born to labor — for Job says, "Man is born to labor" [Job 5.7]. Second, He rebukes the lazy in part because of place since it says, here is a place not of rest but of wandering and vast solitude,[81] as it says in Michea 2, "Arise ye ... for there is no rest here for you" [Mi. 2.10]. Third, He rebukes the lazy in part because of time when he says "all day," that is, according to Job, "Is not man's life on earth a drudgery?" [Job 7.1]. Fourth, He rebukes the lazy in part because of improper action, since "idle" is said. Therefore, Christ clearly grasped these four things, namely: the character indigenous to human nature, the vastness of place, the brevity of time, and the clarity of reason, which prompted [Him to say that] here one should not stand still. And this process must be heeded at all times.

Likewise, it is imperative that in a theme every significant word be divided, so that two meaningful ideas are not subsumed under one division, as for example, if in that theme, "Lord save us, we perish" [Matt. 8.25], it might be said [that] here the apostles do two things: they implore benevolence, because they say, "Lord, save us," and they allege necessity, because they say, "we perish." Since *Lord* is a significant word, it cannot come under any other division. Consequently, it is better to divide in this manner: first, they indicate power in "Lord"; [second,] they implore clemency in "save us"; [third,] they show the need in "we perish."

But when it consists of a single word, the theme as a whole can be set down at the beginning as a division; or it can be subdivided into two, three, or more parts.[82]

For example, let the theme be "Trust!" Here it can be said: one must trust because of three or more reasons. Likewise, if the theme were, "Look around!" Here it can be said that one must look around in six different directions, which are backward to the noble and ignoble who have died, forward to future judgment, to the right to how transitory the good things of the world are, to the left to how familiar the bad things of the world are, downward toward hell, upward toward heaven. Also, if the theme were, "Listen!" Listen, therefore, to Sacred Scripture describing the misery of the present, the penalty of hell, the glory of heaven, about which Ezechiel 2 has, "And there were written in it lamentations and canticles, and woe" [Ezech. 2.9]. "Lamentations" correlates to the "miseries of the present," "canticles" to "glories," "and "woe" [to] Gehenna. Again, if the theme be "Love!" Love God, therefore, in the intellect without error, in speech without contradiction, and in memory without forgetfulness; or thus: love God by glorifying Him, our neighbor by helping him, and yourself by chastising yourself.[83]

Likewise, if the [theme] be two words, it can be divided into two parts, both of which can be subdivided into two, three, or four parts. For example, let the theme be, "Walk in love" [Eph. 5.2]. Here the Apostle does two things: he moves them to set out with "Walk"; second, he shows the correct way with "in love." In regard to the first, one must walk in two manners, or three ways, or four fashions; in regard to the second, one must walk "in love" because the phrase allows for two inspiring segments or because it includes three qualities of the good: [it is] pleasant, useful, and honest. But when the theme has three significant words, a division is appropriately made in three parts, and then the subdivision of each member will be in three parts. If, however, it is divided or subdivided into more parts, that would be burdensome.

Again, regarding division, it must be noted that a theme is able to be divided through verbs thus: in, "Go you also into my vineyard" [Matt. 20.4], here [Christ] does three things: he stirs up, he specifies, and he certifies. He stirs [them] up to acting or setting forth in "Go"; he specifies the object with "into [my] vineyard"; and he certifies the reward when he says, "and what is just" and so forth. And someone [the preacher] will be able, by explication, to direct his division to the second person; thus, according to what is done in Daniel 4 [esp. 19–23]: O Lord, who assumed flesh, "you were glorified"; when then you led us from the pit, "you grew strong"; since from death you arose, "your greatness increased" as you ascended into heaven. Or, for the same text: "You were glorified" in the Incarnation; "you grew strong" in the Passion; "your greatness increased" in the Resurrection.

Likewise, [a theme] can be divided through cases, especially by treating the cases in an orderly fashion as, "Behold, your king comes to thee, meek" [Matt. 21.5]; here three things are in the nominative case: the nearness of the coming in "Behold," the sublimity of the approaching one in "the king," and the usefulness of the arrival in "comes to thee, meek." Again, through the dative case thus: "Art thou he who is to come, or shall we look for another?" [Luke 7.19]. Here two dative structures exist: first, one submits to truth in "Art thou he who is to come?"; second, one is attuned to weakness when "or shall we look for another?" is said. Similarly, in the accusative case as in Malachias 3, "I send my angel" [Mal. 3.1]. Here three things are noted: first, what pertains to the authority of the one sending in "I send"; second, what pertains to the holiness of the deputy in "my angel"; third, what pertains to the dignity of the task in "he shall prepare the way." Likewise, in the ablative case, from Apocalypse 3: "Behold I come … and my reward [is] with me" [Apoc. 22.12]. Here the arrival of the mediator [the God-Man] is developed by a threefold reasoning process: by the nearness of the approaching in "Behold I come"; by the power of giving bountifully in "my reward"; by the equity of the repaying in "to render to every man" and so forth. So, his nearness might urge mankind to hasten; his power might entice to love; his equity might frighten one into being on one's guard.

Chapter XVI: Concerning the "Keys" of Division

At this point, for the clarification of the principal division, certain [preachers] appropriately add a secondary division, which is called the clarification of the parts — or the "key" — because it opens or clarifies the sense of the division; however, it is not necessary to cite an authority for both divisions. For example, let the theme, "Behold we are going up to Jerusalem" [Luke 18.31] be divided thus: here is made known to the disciples the future mystery of the Passion in three respects — as to the time in "we are going" (specifically in the present); as to the place in "Jerusalem"; and as to the result in "all things shall be accomplished." Then, let the division be restated in this manner according to the division of the keys: the time is described by reason of its proximity in "Behold"; the place is described for the purpose of having a common destination in "Jerusalem"; the effect is described in relationship to its expected consequence in "all things shall be accomplished."

Likewise, through external division[84] the theme can be introduced and the key added; thus, if the theme were "Run so as to obtain [the prize]" [I Cor. 9.24], the following can be said: threefold is the law — natural, written and evangelical; of these, the first teaches what must be done, the second what and in what manner it must be done, and the third what, in what manner, and for what purpose it must be done. For that reason, Paul, the preacher of evangelical law, teaches what must be done when he says, "run," in what manner it must be done when he says, "so," and for what purpose it must be done when he says, "as to obtain." The first of those specifies the action, namely, "run"; the second indicates the right way to perform the deed — "so"; and the third guarantees the reward — "as to obtain." Likewise, if the theme were, "I will follow thee, Lord" [Luke 9.61], He must be followed because, as a shepherd He refreshes in times of labor, as a lord He protects in times of temptation, and as a doctor He heals in times of pain. Additionally, if the theme were, "Because of thee we suffer all the day long" [Ps. 43.22], one can speak in this way: penitence is described here in a threefold manner. Indeed, it ought to be undeviating in light of "Because of thee," strong because of "we sufffer," and continuous because of "all the day long." And hence it would be undeviating by reason of intention, strong by reason of action, and continuous by reason of duration. Finally, an authority must be appended for the confirmation of each member unless, by chance, all members can be confirmed by one authority.

Again, there is another method involving, briefly, the division itself and the corresponding key. Hence, if one were to propose this, "I bring you good news of great joy" [Luke 2.10] and so forth, here must be examined first, because of "angel," who "brings good news," surely worthiness; secondly, because of "joy," what is announced, surely usefulness; thirdly, because of "to all the people," to whom the message is brought, surely suitability. By using this method, preachers of old were accustomed to explain and divide into "who," "what," and "how." For example [in], "The just man shall correct me in mercy" [Ps. 140.5] and so forth, here is noted about the judge, what kind of person he should be because of "just man," what he should do because of "shall correct," and how he should do it because of "in mercy." But, modern preachers proceed more subtly by saying: here a judge is described with regard to substance, with regard to act, and with regard to manner. With regard to substance, how he ought to present himself, with regard to act, what he should effect, and with regard to manner, how he should behave.

An explanation can also be made in diverse ways, according to the different modes of knowing; namely, grammatically, philosophically, and logically. For example, grammatically through the verbs, nouns, participles, and adverbs. Thus, if the theme were, "He sent forth his word to heal them" [Ps. 106.20], let it be said that the Word (verb) was active with the father in the creation of all things (hence "the father sent") in order to be passive in the incarnation, "to heal them"; it was neither active nor passive in the flowing forth of blood and water, "and delivered them"; while it was deponent in the release of the fathers, "from their destructions," the Word (verb) was common to all in the last judgment.

Likewise, let the exposition use the tense of the verb, so: would that they knew the past, or understood the present, or foresaw the future. As to the mood of the verb: it will be indicative in the assumption of our nature, imperative in preaching, and subjunctive in our salvation and so forth. Again, let the exposition concentrate on person, so that a theme for the purification can focus on the person of the virgin speaking to Simon: "I will show to thee all good" [Ex. 33.19]. After the division of this verse, one can say: here the courtesy of communication is demonstrated in the first person with "I will show"; in the second person, the abjectness of the arrangement in "to thee"; in the third person, the usefulness of the benefit is signaled in "all good." Similarly, with regard to the participle, let the theme about Mary Magdalene be, "[Mary] has chosen the best part" [Luke 10.42]. Mary was participial in the state of sin, getting a portion of her meaning from a noun, since losing her own name she was called sinner; receiving a portion of her meaning from the verb when at the beginning of her penitence she heard the verb from "Thy sins are forgiven thee" [Luke 7.48]; receiving a portion of her meaning from both [noun and verb] when, for three years, she was lifted up by angelic hands, in part by weeping for her sins and in part by contemplating them.

Likewise, let the preacher make an exposition logically using the parts of the whole taken various ways, either the parts of the whole virtually, or universally, or integrally. Again, an exposition is made philosophically thus: let, "I leave the world and go to the father" [John 16.28] be the theme. In motion three things are required: an end from which, an end to which, and the movement between the ends. As to the first this text says, "I leave the world," as to the movement, it says, "go," and as to the goal, it says, "to the father."

In addition, in a theme using conjunctions, it is possible to proceed thus, as in Romans 13, "Let us lay aside the works of darkness and put on the armor of light" [Rom. 13.12]. Here the Apostle invites us to note two actions, which are the casting off of sins and the putting on of virtues. About the first, two things can be pondered: why sins are called "works of darkness" and why they must be laid aside. Similarly, about the second, two things can be considered: why virtues are called the "armor of light" and why they must be put on.

To this exposition of parts or keys, confirmation by means of an authority must immediately be added. For example, let the theme, "The just man is delivered from trouble" [Prov. 11.8] be divided thus: three things are touched upon: the holiness of the doer, since "the just" is said; the evil of the results, in "from trouble"; the loving kindness of the rescuer in "is delivered." This is made clear by a confirming authority. In regard to holiness, the exemplary way of life is the first step, expressed in "the just" of Proverbs, "The path of the just is like a shining light that grows in brilliance" [Prov. 4.18]. In regard to evil, exceptional distress compounds the "from trouble," as in Job, "[The darkness] fills him with dread; distress and trouble overpower him" [Job 15.24]. In regard to loving kindness, intimate love is demonstrated in the end by "is delivered," as in Timothy 2, "The Lord will deliver me from every work of evil" [II Tim. 4.18].

Chapter XVII: About the Amplification [Dilation] of the Sermon

Here it must be noted that amplification is accomplished in two ways: through the subdivision of the parts and through the exposition of the cited authority. For example, in setting forth and dividing this theme, “The young man will dwell with the virgin” [Is. 62.5], one can comment as follows: concerning a virgin, one must know that a certain kind must be detested, another imitated, and another admired. To be detested is the one who is not consecrated to God, but is honored for her vainglory, about which it is said in Sacred Scripture, “Her virgins are foul” [Lam. 1.4]. But, if to corroborate this an example or adaptation or authority is brought forth, so much the better. Virginity is to be imitated which is consecrated to God, for just as virgins follow their parents (by whom they are protected) to church, so those who have presented their virginity to God follow Him by whom they are guarded, whence in the Apocalypse is said, “These are they who were not defiled with women, for they are virgins. These follow the lamb” [Apoc. 14.4]. The third kind of virginity, which does not have an equal, is to be admired, namely, where there is virginity together with fecundity — which is met with only in the Blessed Mary — whence in Ecclesiasticus is found, “Motherlike she will meet him, like a young bride [she will embrace him]” [Eccli. 15.2], and in Luke 1 is said, “The angel Gabriel was sent” [Luke 1.26] and so forth. Observe how in this method of dividing, the first subject [the hypocritical virgin] is dealt with in the form of a command, the second [the one dedicated to God] is recommended, and the third [the Virgin Mary] is surpassingly excellent.

Moreover, a subdivision can be made so that, at the end of whatever member has been recommended, its contrary is opposed [to it]; Brother Nicholas used this procedure in his *Distinctiones*, which begin with the word “abeuncium”[85] and Blessed Augustine [also] in his *Expositiones*, where he says: “On the other hand it is said about the wicked.”[86] And that method is very useful for the people because it lends itself productively to commending virtues and reproving vices. For example, about a virgin, there appear to be three favorable qualities, which, are [first,] the ornament of grace, as is said in Jeremias, “Will [a virgin] forget her ornament?” [Jer. 2.32]; but, on the other hand, this verse in the Bible, “Her virgins are foul” [Lam. 1,4]. Secondly, she is said to have the defense of modesty, as in Genesis, “The young woman [was] very beautiful, a virgin undefiled” [Gen. 24.16], which is the opposite of the daughter of Jepthe, who, crossing the mountains, lamented her virginity.[87] Thirdly, she ought to have the seasoning of love according to that verse in Matthew 25, “[The wise] did take oil in their vessels with the lamps” [Matt. 25.4], which is the contrary of the foolish maidens lacking oil.

[In addition,] by this method, the preacher can subdivide the second and third members into three parts and in that way there is a threefold manner of proceeding because, initially, the three members of the first section can be explained, then, the three members of the second section, and finally, the three members of the third section. Thus, first are discussed the three kinds of virgins, second, the three kinds of youthfulness, and third, the three kinds of dwelling.[88] At this point it would be appropriate if in the last member of the first division one were able to introduce the second main division, and in the last member of the second main division one were able to introduce the third main division, as if there were a kind of continuity or juncture [created] by means of one authority in which the first and second members would be found and, again, by another authority in which the second and third members would be found.

Likewise, another method is through a correspondence of the members with each other so that the first member of the first division is conformed to the second member of the second, and to the third member of the third; or, the second member of the first to the second member of the second, and to the second member of the third; and again, the third member of the first to the third member of the second, and to the third member of the third. But this curiosity of circular correspondence is not very useful for the people. Certain preachers cleverly subdivide by separating the first member into three parts, the second into two, and the third into one, which remains undivided so that the sermon is virtually in the shape of a pyramid, that is, having a wide base extending upward to a single point.[89] If, however, the sermon should have two or three members without further division, it is called a linear sermon since it is in the form of a line, having only one division. This method is clear and useful for the people. [In it, though,] much emphasis must be put on the exposition of cited authorities, since no other subdivision exists to expand the sermon. However, if [in another sermon structure] the subdivision of the first member should be extensive, then the preacher may omit dealing with the subdivision of the other members, which the conclusion of the sermon always touches on.[90] At the end, let eternal reward be requested.

Chapter XVIII: About Subdivision of the Various Parts

About the method of subdivision, here it must be noted that in as many ways as division is accomplished, so is subdivision. Moreover, according to Boethius in his *Liber de divisione*, division is achieved in six ways.[91] Primarily, the universal is divided into subordinate parts, which are differentiated into genus and species, as if blessedness were divided into blessedness in reality and blessedness in hope. Then, there is the division of the complete whole into its integral parts, so blessedness in reality consists in union with God and in the enjoyment of God.[92] Again division is made according to the significations of words, so if, "The temple of the Lord" is stated, according to the literal sense, this signifies the temple of Solomon, which was constructed from wood and stone; according to the allegorical sense, it denotes Blessed Mary or the Church militant; according to the tropological sense, it signifies the Christian soul or conscience; according to the anagogical sense, it denotes the Church triumphant.[93] Fourthly, division is made of subjects into accidents, so it might be said that customarily, according to our writings, some men are innocent, some are penitent, and some are perfect. Fifthly, division is made of accidents into subjects, so of the saints, some are apostles, some are angels. Sixthly, division is made of accidents into accidents, so of the saints, some are martyrs, some are confessors. To these modes, a seventh can be added in which a potential whole is divided into its potential parts, so it might be said that the blood of Christ must restore from original sin, must cleanse from actual sin, and must redeem from infernal punishment.[94]

If, therefore, you wish to subdivide some member, consider the meaning of the section and the reason for subdividing, and see if you are able first to subdivide into subordinate parts. If not, then attempt to subdivide by integral parts and so on from there until you are able to find some division appropriate to your text in which the members of the subdivision do not repeat themselves nor are too multiple; also be sure one member follows from another and, if possible, that the members relate rhetorically. So, for example, we ought to traverse the road of penitence by detesting sin, the road of patience by tolerating adversity, the road of justice by rendering to each what is his. However, in preaching, that division which pertains to the significations of words is not always useful, since this process is more relevant to those who are disputing about logical fallacies and to those who are studying in the schools about the explanation of contraries, rather than to those who are preaching.[95]

Chapter XIX: Concerning Amplification made through Authorities

A sermon can be amplified in many ways. One method involves making a statement in place of a word, as occurs in definitions, descriptions, explanations, and other comparable observations. For example, let the theme be, The Lord "conducted the just through the right ways"[96] or, "The just man shall flourish like the palm tree" [Ps. 91.13]; "the just man" is described as follows: by [what he does] — renders to everyone what is rightly his — and by how he renders it — to God as to a superior, to his equal as to himself, and to his inferior as to a neighbor. Moreover, when something is defined or described, the preacher will be able to apply his discussion to a different but related concept since the exposition of the former can lead to the understanding of the latter. And so, having described one virtue, the preacher can proceed to other virtues thus: as justice is shown in rendering to everyone what is rightly his, so prudence is shown in understanding, fortitude is shown in enduring, and so forth. In this method of amplifying, it is appropriate to seek out descriptions and explanations, because an exposition is sometimes more applicable to one subject than to another. When applying this method, the preacher must avoid obscurity for, according to

Boethius, descriptions, definitions, and interpretations are presented for the sake of imparting knowledge.[97]

The second method of amplifying is through divisions [and] as Porphyry says, it is necessary in dividing to consider a multitude of things.[98] For example, if the text for discussion is, "Virtue is made perfect in weakness" [II Cor. 12.9], it is subdivided in this way: some virtues are labeled cardinal, some theological, and so forth. In the former we relate to our neighbor, in the latter to God. Concerning this topic, refer to the previous chapter.

The third method of amplifying is through reasoning or persuading, which happens, chiefly, in three ways. The first occurs when, with regard to any two things, it is determined to approve one and to disapprove the other. For example, if I intend to approve continence, I say: lechery destroys wealth, the body, the soul, and one's reputation; therefore continence, which is its contrary, must be embraced. Another method is to continue through a hidden enthymeme by asking for a judgment from the listeners themselves. For example, would not one be foolish who, with his own hands, weaves a rope with which he may be hanged by his enemy? Such is the sinner, as is said in Proverbs 4, each person is tied up by the rope of his sins.[99] The prophet Nathan used this method against David, and Christ himself used it in parables about farmers, as is seen in Matthew.[100]

The fourth method of amplifying is to argue by means of examples. For instance, the apostles and martyrs endured many tribulations to reach the kingdom; this is necessary for us as well. Also, take advantage of antitheses and refutations which can be used in responding to silent objections. Thus, whoever should wish to show that the incarnation of God's son was necessary should argue against himself: could not the world have been redeemed by a pure man? For if a pure man sinned, a pure man should have made satisfaction.[101] But to this statement one can respond that it is greater to re-create than create, or at least it is not any less great. If, therefore, it was necessary that the Creator be God, how much more necessary was it that the Re-creator be God. But, in this method, let the preacher beware of raising an issue unless he can clearly solve it. Also let him beware, lest he so commend the greater good that he seem rather to despise the lesser good. In regard to this, see above, chapter five.[102]

The fifth method of amplifying is through parallel passages which correspond in word (as, "Blessed is the *man* who endures temptations" [James 1.12], about which is said in Job 38, "Gird up your loins … like a *man*" [Job 38.3]), or in meaning although not in word (as in Colossians 2, "Faith without works is *dead*" [James 2.20], about which it is said in Genesis 34, "Rachel said to Jacob: 'Give me children, or I shall *die*'" [Gen. 30.1]). Faith is symbolized by Rachel and works done with love are symbolized by her children. Another variation occurs when one authority says explicitly what another authority says implicitly. Thus it is said, "So run as to obtain [the prize]"

[I Cor. 9.24]. How the running must be done is defined in the psalm, "Without iniquity have I run, and I directed [my steps]" [Ps. 58.5], and elsewhere in a psalm, "I will run the way of your commands" [Ps. 118.32].

The sixth method of amplifying occurs when those words stemming from the same root are expounded through the grades of comparison. For example [in], "Gird your sword ... O mighty one" [Ps. 44.4], some people are girded powerfully, that is, those who are married; some, more powerfully, that is, those who are chaste; some, most powerfully, that is, virgins. Another example is, "Drink, most dear ones" [Cant. 5.1]. The dear are beginners and imperfect; the dearer are those more advanced who suffer misfortunes for Christ, but do so with annoyance; the most dear are those who, as if drunk, laugh amid scorn. Related to this method is amplification through the use of compounds [of the same base word]. For example, if the text is, "Seek (*querite*) his face always" [Ps. 104.4], it is able to be said that God is sought (*queritur*) in baptism, sought again (*requirtur*) in penitence, sought carefully (*inquiritur*) in meditating on the commandments, sought diligently (*exquiritur*) in doing good, and, finally, reached (*adquiritur*) in the heavenly homeland.

The seventh method consists in explaining metaphors by means of the properties of things. For example, The just man grows like a lily.[103] Here, the properties of the lily are stated and it is explained that a just man is compared to it because as the lily is white and fragrant and grows near the water, so a just man is shining white in abstinence, fragrant in good reputation, and makes progress through the waters of tribulation as did the Sons of Israel who, the more they were oppressed by the pharaoh, the more they flourished. In this method, the preacher must not immediately change the metaphor by shifting to the characteristics of other things, but he can move to the subordinate parts of the same universal or to the integral parts of the same whole. So, if the theme were, "I am the flower of the field" [Cant. 2.1], the sermon can be made about a rose, about a lily, or about similar flowers since Christ was a lily in the Nativity, a rose during the Passion, and a violet in the Tomb. At this point, it is not a good idea to speak of Christ as a shepherd or a rock, but if the theme were, "I am the good shepherd" [John 10.11], the sermon could be made about a shepherd in relationship to the sheepfold, the sheep, the ram, the dogs, the helpful or worthless servants, or even the wolf — not the wolf per se as an animal, but as a hunter of sheep and one who undermines the shepherd's work because the same methodology applies to contraries. One can deal, likewise, with integral parts; so if the theme were, "We are members of one another" [Eph. 4.25], it would not be wrong if one showed how one member is helpful to another: the eye in foreseeing, the arm in defending, the foot in moving forward, the nostrils in forewarning or sensing, the tongue in informing.

The eighth method of amplifying explains the theme according to the different senses of Scripture: historical, allegorical, tropological, and anagogical. History, of course, is the narrative of deeds; allegory occurs when through one thing, another is signified, so the fact that David conquered Goliath signifies Christ conquering the devil; tropology results when one action points to the doing of another, and consequently that David conquered Goliath suggests that the faithful man ought to overcome the devil; anagogy exists when what is done in the Church militant indicates a future happening in the Church triumphant, as is shown in the multifaceted mystery of the temple by which the Church triumphant is signified, just as the tabernacle of Moses denotes the Church militant.[104] Concerning all this, for example, if "Jerusalem, built as a city" [Ps. 121.3], is quoted, here "Jerusalem" literally refers to a certain terrestrial city, allegorically, to the Church militant, morally or tropologically to the soul of the faithful, anagogically to the Church triumphant. Also, one must note that not all allegories are about Christ; they can also refer to Sacred Scripture, the Church, its members and constituencies, like Jews, pagans, and saints.[105] Likewise, when using this method of amplifying, one must consider the weight of the words: why this particular word and not another, why in such a manner and not otherwise. For example, in, "This day I have begotten you" [Ps. 2.7], the "I" (*ego*) is stated separately [separately from the verb] as if to say, "not someone else." And since the substance of the first person refers to the Father, one properly says "begotten" (*genui*), not "created" (*creavi*) or "made" (*feci*). One also properly says "this day" (*hodie*), not "yesterday" (*heri*) nor "tomorrow" (*cras*), nor "at night" (*nocte*). [Likewise] "you" (*te*) because I [God] have made you eternally, not "thine" (*tua*) which I [God] have made temporally.

The ninth method of amplifying is to proceed through causes and effects, assigning the necessary and essential causes. For in speaking about a cause, one can switch over to its opposite and vice versa. For example, if the theme is, "Humble yourself ... under the mighty hand of God" [I Pet. 5.6], a sermon can be made about the causes of humiliation, which are the imperfections of our body and soul in light of the contemplation of another's perfection; and after this, the effects of humility are able to be designated, which are that it illuminates, preserves, and exalts.

The tenth method of amplifying is through digression, which means that something incidental — outside the ordinary compass of the principal point — is discussed, as long as it is not too remote from the principal point. For example, if it is said about John the Evangelist that he was considered a second son by the Mother [Mary] because of his great purity, then one can add:

> Therefore, woe to the soul which contemplates so many illustrations of purity and yet does not imitate them, since in almost every church is depicted Christ the virgin, with his Mother the virgin on the right and John the virgin at the left.[106] These three are put in a place on high to be imitated, at least in chastity if not in virginity. Hence, in light of such a powerful example, whoever neglects the angelic life, scorns the [proper] status of man, and wallows in pleasure certainly can expect damnation — and perhaps without

warning. So it has happened to many, for it says in Proverbs 22, "Ruin [draws nigh] to the evil man" [Prov. 12.13]. Indeed, the evil man possesses a foretaste of his ruin in the present life, as much through remorse as through the struggle of his conscience. He samples something now which after death he will drink in full, according to Boethius in his *Consolation of Philosophy*: pleasure possesses that which goads its devotees with spurs and so forth.[107] But, possessing purity with John, one avoids the previously mentioned ill-effects, according to that text of Proverbs, "The just man is delivered from trouble" [Prov. 12.13].

Chapter XX: About the Rules for Dilation

In bringing forward for consideration authorities to support the theme, [note that] there are various verbal structures by which an authority is able to be introduced. For example, if we want to persuade people that they ought not to love earthly things, rather [to love] heavenly things, and we wish to cite this passage of the Apostle, "For ... now [I] tell you that they are enemies of the cross of Christ whose bellies are their God" [Phil. 3.18] and so forth, let us speak in this manner:

> Brothers, we ought not delight excessively in earthly things like those who care only about the gluttony of their stomach. Therefore, because such people are unduly dedicated to earthly things, deservedly are they called enemies of Christ, according to that text of the Apostle, "For ... now [I] tell you that they are enemies of the cross of Christ" and so forth.

And, if all the members are able to be confirmed through one authority, this would be good. For example, let the theme for the Assumption be, "Today she is lifted up" [I Mac. 2.63], as is said in the first book of Maccabees.[108] Here two things are notable: the coincidence of the time is appropriately captured in "today," and high honor is conferred upon the Virgin in the words "is lifted up." From these two things that line in Joshua 3 can be cited, "Today I will begin to exalt you in the sight of all Israel" [Jos. 3.7].

Again, another rule is that if the vocabulary is in Greek or Hebrew, it ought to be explained or interpreted; one must have recourse to the meaning which best suits the point being made. Thus "Jacob," which is interpreted "Supplantor,"[109] designates the penitent who has to supplant the threefold enemy: the world, the flesh, and the devil.[110]

Yet another rule pertains to the exposition of Sacred Scripture, as follows: this exposition ought to be tempered so that it does not contradict too obviously the literal meaning of the text, nor the articles of faith, nor the already accepted truth.

Likewise, another rule obtains since preaching is of three kinds (discussed previously in chapter 7),[111] namely: that for Sundays, for feast days, and for the various situations of men. When a Sunday sermon is given, the theme should be taken from the Gospel or the Epistle; and if it is from the Gospel, before one gets down to pursuing the theme, the evangelist's account should be narrated and then the individual virtues discussed, just as the parts of the Gospel demand. However, if the feast of some well-known saint falls on a Sunday, those things which should otherwise be said about moral actions ought to be applied in detail to the saint himself, and this will serve to edify the listeners. But, if the saint's feast day falls on Ash Wednesday, or Easter, or on solemn vigils like that for the Nativity of the Lord, or on Pentecost, the sermon is to be fashioned according to the liturgical season and then adapted to the saint. When, however, the sermon is created solely about a particular saint, let the treatment be principally about the saint's life and incidentally about moral behavior; for example, if the theme were, "It is the Passover of the Lord,"[112] it should be divided thus: initially, the condition or quality of Resurrection is noted in "Passover," which is interpreted "passing over"; secondly, the authority or jurisdiction of the Risen One [is noted in] "of the Lord"; [finally,] the veracity of the Resurrection is manifested to the world by "is," which is a significant word and an expression of truth. This division proceeds in this manner: at the outset, it is noted here that "Passover" is the same as "to make a transition," and in this time the Lord achieves a threefold transition: bread is changed into his body;[113] our death is destroyed through his sacrifice; his body is regained after death. The first of these occurred during the Last Supper when Christ instituted the Eucharist; the second happened during Passover when he overcame the devil on the Cross; and the third is actualized today since Christ has brought the reality of resurrection to us. And so, we too should "pass over" in a triplex manner: first, from the miseries of sins, so that we are refreshed by the sacraments; second, from the desires of the flesh, so that we are one with Christ's sufferings; third, with our souls stripped of earthly delights, so that we may enjoy the fruits of happiness. However, if one were to preach about some particular condition [of people], let that situation be effectively presented through figures of speech, examples from the Bible or lives of the saints, through comparisons with visible things, or through some miraculous occurrence which relates to that condition.

There are other rules of modern preachers which [state] that not more than three figures of speech, three stories, or three examples be cited in one sermon, so that a single significant member contains not more than one figure of speech, one example, and one story. Others are accustomed to proving their proposition in a threefold manner, namely by authority, by reason, and by example, according to that text in Wisdom, "A three-ply cord is not easily broken" [Eccl. 4.12]. Others now strive to illustrate this in a triple, beautifully colored manner through a proof from Scripture, through an illustration from nature, and through a figure of speech. Still others illustrate through irrefutable argument, through infallible demonstration, and through sensory example. Whence, if it is right to confirm one statement through an example from nature, it would be right to confirm another statement through an example from art; and, according to Augustine, if occasionally an authority is lacking for demonstrating proof, one must use reason, without which no authority has any validity.[114]

Chapter XXI: Concerning Coloration of the Various Parts

The sermon is colored in two ways: through similar word endings or through a similar syllabic pattern. The first is used in the antetheme, in the theme, and in the subdivision of the theme, as well as at the end of clauses. The second is appropriate everywhere.

Concerning the first, note that sometimes similarity is achieved by means of one syllable.[115] Thus, if the theme were, "The just man shall correct me in mercy" [Ps. 140.5], a prelate is described with respect to station ("stat*um*"): "just man"; with respect to action ("act*um*"): "shall correct"; with respect to manner ("mod*um*"): "in mercy." Sometimes, the coloring is achieved by means of two syllables, as if in the same theme is said: here it is shown how a prelate should comport himself ("stat*um* exhibe*re*"): as a "just man"; what action he should demonstrate ("act*um* exerce*re*"): "shall correct"; what manner he should possess ("mod*um* tene*re*"): "in mercy." The same process occurs when the coloring is achieved by means of three syllables, thus: his status, prudently described ("stat*us* pruden*ter* preliban*dus*") is first mentioned: "just man"; his action, to be exercised frequently ("act*us* frequen*ter* exercen*dus*") is added: "shall correct"; and finally, his manner, tempered with forebearance ("mod*us* clemen*ter* moderan*dus*") is explained: "in mercy." This type of coloration is focused on the character of the words.

The other method, focused on metrics, is called cadence and can be found, not only where there is a simple pause like a comma, but also at a moderate pause like a semicolon, and at a full stop, which is what occurs at the end of a sentence.[116] Indeed, this cadence, formerly used in a multifold manner, is practiced by modern preachers in three ways. The first of these is called dactylic because it contains two dactyls, that is, six syllables arranged in two dactyls as in *francis origine*. The second cadence has a dactyl and a spondee as in *genere francus*. The third has one dactyl and two spondees as in *schemate generoso*.[117] The first of these cadences is put, more appropriately, in the first part [of a sentence]; the second, in the second part and/or in the middle distinction [midpoint of a sentence].[118] And the third can be placed anywhere, although it is better put at the end.

THE ART OF COMPOSING SERMONS IS FINISHED. NOTE THAT, SEQUENTIALLY, THE INITIAL LETTERS IN EACH CHAPTER OF THIS ART SPELL OUT: *ARS RANULPHI CESTRENSIS*.[119]

Notes

[1] The section between "When skillfully making sermons" and "CHAPTER I" functions in part like an *accessus* to the *Ars componendi sermones*. It lists the *Ars*' contents and discusses a theme's appropriateness and applicability — both items of interest to Ranulph Higden — but it also emphasizes the necessity for a theme's completeness in "word and sense," a focus not characteristic of the treatise as a whole. Sentence structure patterns and vocabulary suggest that this section was not written by Higden. It has been translated here, however, because it appears in three of the five surviving manuscripts.
[2] A biblical sentiment related to Dan. 3.38 and Ps. 50.18, but not verbally equatable to either text.
[3] Both theoretical and practical definitions of preaching are embraced here. It is public persuasion in the broadest (and classical) sense as noted earlier by Alain de Lille (PL 210: 111), but it is also defined by reason of its structure as manifested in the many treatises attributed to John of Wales; see Margaret Jennings, "The Preacher's Rhetoric: The *Ars componendi sermones* of Ranulph Higden," in *Medieval Eloquence*, ed. James J. Murphy (Berkeley: University of California Press, 1978), pp. 112–26, at pp. 114–15.
[4] John's Gospel records this story at length; see John 4.1–42.
[5] The Aristotelian four causes were defined and illustrated in a variety of medieval venues. They appear frequently in the introductory matter of commentaries, for example, and are found in arts of preaching by Basevorn, James of Fusignano, Martin of Cordoba and several other manualists. See several relevant contributions in *Les prologues médiévaux. Actes du colloque international organisé par l'Academia Belgica et l'École française de Rome avec le concours de la F.I.D.E.M. (Rome, 26–28 mars 1998)*, ed. Jacqueline Hamesse, Textes et études du moyen âge 15 (Turnhout: Brepols, 2000). See also John O. Ward, *Ciceronian Rhetoric in Treatise, Scholion and Commentary* (Turnhout: Brepols, 1995), pp. 70–71, and Margaret Jennings' dissertation, *The Ars componendi sermones of Ranulph Higden* (Bryn Mawr, 1970), p. 170 n. 180.
[6] Ranulph could be referring to a local domestic difficulty but, since he was a renowned historian probably functioning as head of St. Werburgh's scriptorium, such an explanation seems unlikely. It is possible, because the area in front of the abbey was used for performances and because Chester seems to have been in the early stages of developing its Whitsun plays in the fourteenth century, that the comment refers to a developed liturgical Resurrection play where a highly dramatized purveyor of oil interacts with the Three Marys. See David Mills, *Recycling the Cycle: The City of Chester and its Whitsun Plays* (Toronto: University of Toronto Press, 1998), pp. 27–8; *The Chester Mystery Cycle*, ed. R. M. Lumiansky and David Mills, Early English Texts Society, S.S. 9 (Oxford: Oxford University Press, 1986), vol. 2, p. 287; and Karl Young, *The Drama of the Medieval Church* (Oxford: Clarendon Press, 1933), vol. 1, pp. 401–5, 423, 435, and vol. 2, p. 366.
[7] The Canon Law citation here is the most extensive found in this text, although such references are commonplace in Higden's *Speculum curatorum*. Stephanie Tibbetts, of the Institute of Medieval Canon Law, identifies it as stemming from the *Decretum Gratiani*, hypothetical case XI, in chap. 86 of the third question (beginning with "nolite"); so: Causa XI, q. iii, c. 86, "nolite" (in *Corpus Iuris Canonici*, ed. Emil Friedberg, 2 vols. [Leipzig: Tauchnitz, 1879], vol. 1, col. 667). The "extra" refers to the compilation of decretals made by Gregory IX in 1234, called by canonists the *Liber extra*. "Quod metus causa" is an alternate and truncated title of the section "De hiis, quae vi metusve causa fiunt"; the chapter beginning "sacris" is located there at I.xl.5. See *CIC*, ed. Friedberg, vol. 2, col. 220. The *Super Mattheum*, spuriously attributed to St. John Chrysostom, is found more frequently in medieval libraries than any of his other works. See R. M. Wilson, "The Contents of the Mediaeval Library," in *The English Library Before 1700*, ed. Francis Wormald and C. E. Wright (London: Athlone Press, 1958), pp. 85–111, at p. 89.
[8] The prophet is Isaias, whose "vinum tuum mixtum est aqua" (to which Ranulph probably refers) appears in 1.22. The verse is also discussed in the *Decretum Gratiani*, distinctio 86, chapter 5, in *CIC*, ed. Friedberg, vol. 1, col. 299.

[9] Augustine, *De doctrina christiana*, II, 151. Should a reader wish to review the context of Ranulph's references, their volume and column number in J. P. Migne's *Patrologia Latina* or the appropriate page(s) in a standard bibliographical source will be appended; here, *De doctrina christiana*, ed. and trans. R. P. H. Green (Oxford: Clarendon Press, 1995), pp. 128–9. N.B.: many of the treatises cited exist in several modern editions.

[10] Jerome, *Adversus Iovinianum*, Book I, chap. 1–49 passim (PL 23: 241–333). A representative portion of Jerome's treatise has been printed in *Jankyn's Book of Wikked Wyves*, ed. Ralph Hanna and Traugott Lawlor (Athens: University of Georgia Press, 1997), pp. 157–93 and 231–258.

[11] Gregory the Great, *XL Homiliarum in evangelia*, Book I, homily 12 (PL 76: 919–34).

[12] This statement is also discussed in the *Decretum Gratiani*, Causa III, q. vii, c. 27, in *CIC*, ed. Friedberg, vol. 1, col. 526. There is no section headed "Nullus" in the fortieth distinction, although a discussion about how one's life rather than one's title merits God's approbation is contained there; see ibid., col. 146–7. Distinction LX does have entries under "Nullus"; Ranulph may have conflated the two citations.

[13] Socrates Scholasticus, *Ecclesiastica historia,* Book I, chap. 20, ed. Robert Hussey (Oxford: Oxford University Press, 1853; reprinted, Hildesheim: Georg Olms, 1992), pp. 117–23. The book's title has not been translated to avoid its being confused with Bede's *Ecclesiastical History.*

[14] Gregory the Great, *Moralium liber XIX in caput XXVIII beati Job*, chap. 30 (PL 76: 134–6).

[15] Gregory the Great, *Regulae pastoralis liber*, Book III, chap. 40 (PL 77: 124). The equation of the rooster (cock) and the preacher was commonplace in the Middle Ages, as shown in Durandus' *Rationale divinorum officiorum*, I, 22; see Beryl Rowland, *Birds with Human Souls* (Knoxville: University of Tennessee Press, 1978), pp. 21–2. In many religious traditions, a cockcrow also routs devils; see Pierre Boglioni, "Les animaux dans l'hagiographie monastique," in *L'animal exemplaire au moyen âge*, ed. Jacques Berlioz *et al.* (Rennes: Presses universitaires, 1999), pp. 51–80, at p. 77.

[16] Aristotle, *Nicomachean Ethics*, IV, vii, 2–17; see the Loeb Classical Library edition (Cambridge, MA: Harvard University Press, 1962), pp. 242–5.

[17] Valerius Maximus, *Facta et dicta memorabilia liber,* 8.10.2, ed. John Briscoe (Stutgart: Teubner, 1998), vol. 2, p. 537.

[18] From chapter xii of Hugh of St. Victor's *De institutione novitiorum* (PL 176: 948).

[19] Augustine, *De doctrina christiana*, IV, 104 (see above, n. 9), pp. 244–5.

[20] Epistle 100, section 10 in L. Annaeus Seneca, *Ad Lucilium epistolae morales*, ed. L. D. Reynolds (Oxford: Clarendon Press, 1965), vol. 2, p. 419.

[21] Bede, *Expositio actuum apostolorum et retractatio*, ed. M. L. W. Laistner (Cambridge, MA: Mediaeval Academy Publications, 1939), XIV, vii, p. 59. The proverbial overtones are probably less important than the biblical ones (from Gen. 7, II Kings 23.4, and Amos 4.7).

[22] Gregory the Great, *XL Homiliarum in Ezechielem*, Book I, homily 21 (PL 76: 906–19).

[23] Gregory the Great *Moralium Liber XXIV in caput XXXIV beati Job* (PL 76: 316).

[24] These references to physicians and farmers correspond with comments in Gregory the Great's *XL Homiliarum in Ezechielem*, Book I, homily 9 (PL 76: 913–14), which Ranulph had just cited.

[25] Gregory the Great, *Moralium liber XXX in caput XXXVIII beati Job*, chap. 3 (PL 76: 527–8).

[26] Gregory the Great, *Regulae pastoralis Liber*. Part III, prologue (PL 77: 49).

[27] Ibid., chap. 36 (PL 77: 121–2).

[28] Gregory the Great, *Regulae pastoralis liber*, Part III, chap. 39 (PL 77: 124).

[29] The cause and effect situation described in Exodus 34.30–5 is related to, but not identical with, Ranulph's statement.

[30] Job 26.8 says "he binds up water in his clouds." Job is replying to his friends Bildad of Shuh or Zophar of Naamath about the dimensions of God's power.

[31] Addressing the various penchants of people was already a concern in the sixth century; Gregory's *Regulae pastoralis liber*, Part III (PL 77: 49–121) talks at length about how a preacher should tailor his words to the predilections of his audience. In the later Middle Ages, this concern was specified as the need to preach an appropriate sermon to the different types, classes, and situations of people. Jacques de Vitry (ca. 1160–1240), a well known author and cleric, distinguished 120 categories of hearers and thus oriented his *Sermones vulgares* (or *Sermones ad status*); see the edition of Jean Baptiste Pitra, *Analecta novissima spicilegii Solesmensis, altera continuatio* (Paris: Roger et Chernowitz, 1885–88), vol. 2. In the *artes praedicandi*, comments about "sermones ad status" are to be found from Alain de Lille onward. An extreme case is that of the fourteenth-century Munich ms. 14550, fols. 97–114, which, though styled an "art of preaching," discusses only a sermon's effects "ad varios status," giving no technical advice about structure.

[32] Ecclesiastical and/or monastic interests are reflected in this list: "visitations" are periodic inspections of the temporal and spiritual affairs of a monastery or a diocese; "elections" in the Benedictine tradition are held to choose an abbot, the leader of each monastery; "synods" are formal meetings of bishops and representatives of several churches convened for the purpose of regulating doctrine or discipline; "processions" could take place before the celebration of the Eucharist or after Vespers; sometimes held in the open air as acts of witness, they may be penitential or festal or petitional. See E. A. Livingstone, *The Concise Oxford Dictionary of the Christian Church* (Oxford: Oxford University Press, 1977), pp. 541 (visitation), 1 (abbot), 132 (diocesan synod), 417 (procession).

[33] By 1346, word of a pestilence of unprecedented fury had reached Europe and records of its destruction are available starting in October, 1347. Called the "Black Death," it arrived in England about September, 1348 and in subsequent years caused massive social readjustment as more than a third of the population perished; see John Arberth, *From the Brink of Apocalypse* (New York: Routledge, 2001), passim and Colin Platt, *King Death: The Black Death and it Aftermath in Late Medieval England* (Toronto: University of Toronto Press, 1997), pp. 5–9. The detached nature of Ranulph's comment implies that the *Ars*' date of composition is 1346–47; the plague was a known entity, but it had not yet struck England or Ranulph's monastery, whose abbot died of it in 1349, according to Philip Ziegler, *The Black Death* (New York: John Day, 1969), p. 189.

[34] Thomas Waleys, in the second chapter of his *De modo componendi sermones*, explains that this text, based on Genesis 18, is actually one of the responsories for Sundays during Eastertime; see T. M. Charland, *Artes praedicandi* (Ottawa: Institut d'études médiévales, 1936), p. 342. Responsories, regularly used in the Divine Office after the lessons, are liturgical chants designed for alternate singing; see Livingstone, *The Concise Oxford Dictionary of the Christian Church* (as in n. 32), p. 436. Genesis 18.2–3 reads: "And when he raised his eyes he saw three men standing at a distance from him. As soon as he saw them he ran from the entrance of the tent door to meet them, and bowed down to the earth, and said, 'My Lord' ..."

[35] The conflation here of Cant. 6.10, Cant. 5.1, and Eccli. 24.42 undermines the lesson.

[36] Lines 9–12 of Venantius Fortunatus' "Vexilla regis prodeunt," sung at First Vespers on Passion Sunday and attributed to Ambrose during the medieval period; see *The Oxford Book of Medieval Latin Verse*, ed. F. J. E. Raby (Oxford: Clarendon Press, 1961), p. 75.

[37] Fear of heresy was endemic in the Middle Ages; see Malcolm Lambert, *Medieval Heresy* (Oxford: Blackwell, 1992).

[38] Omitting the "and" seems to give the Magdalene a volitional power not consonant with the incident recounted in Luke 8.2.

[39] Ranulph apparently used Basevorn's *Forma praedicandi* without checking the biblical text which agrees that Tryphon was evil, but which clearly says, "And when Tryphon understood that Simon was risen up in the place of his brother Jonathan ..." (I Mac. 13.14).

[40] When scholastic writers and/or copyists wished to indicate that a word was being discussed qua word, they placed the letters "li" or "ly" before it. The letters have no translatable meaning but, since they are intended to capture the reader's attention by highlighting a verbal entity, I have italicized the words thus signaled. In this instance, Ranulph points to the disparate meanings of the verb "intendo"; in Ps. 10.3, a physical bending is indicated, whereas Ps. 140.1 and Ps. 62.9 refer to a psychological inclination.

[41] The first sermon in the collection of Jacobus de Voragine's *Sermones de sanctis per anni circulum*, published at Pavia in 1499, seems to fit Ranulph's description; the text appears in Thomas Kaeppeli, O. P., *Scriptores Ordinis Praedicatorum Medii Aevi* (Rome: St. Sabina, 1970–93), vol. 2, #2155.

[42] Using the names of the apostles to give definition to twelve-part units was commonplace in the Middle Ages; see James D. Gordon, "The Articles of the Creed and the Apostles," *Speculum* 40 (1965), pp. 634–40. In his *Speculum curatorum*, Ranulph identified fourteen credal statements and solved this problem by assigning the first three to Peter; see MS. Balliol College 77, fols. 3v–4r.

[43] Probably Guy d'Evreux, whose renowned collection of sermons, completed about 1293, was often described as a *Summa sermonum dominicalium*. Guy treated the theme and protheme as two separate elements of the sermon, connected only by a common word; see Pierre Michaud-Quantin, "Guy d'Evreux, O.P., technicien du sermonnaire médiéval," *Archivum Fratrum Praedicatorum* 20 (1950), pp. 213–33.

[44] Gregory the Great, *XL Homiliarum in evangelia*, Book II, homily 30 (PL 76: 1219–27).

[45] Ranulph is copying directly from Basevorn in this passage; see Charland, *Artes praedicandi* (as in n. 34), pp. 256–7. Nevertheless, the word "Gloss" requires explication. Inserted interlinearly or marginally, a gloss is a translation, explanation, or interpretation of a word or passage. Glosses were most commonly used to clarify passages in Canon Law, although they were also developed to explain material from the Hebrew and Christian scriptures. By the twelfth century, a cadre of scholars, under Anslem of Laon, had gathered together fragments of commentary from diverse people and places and formed them into the popular and lengthy *Glossa ordinaria*; see Beryl Smalley, *The Study of the Bible in the Middle Ages* (Notre Dame: University of Notre Dame Press, 1964), pp. 46–66 and, more recently, Karlfried Froehlich and Margaret T. Gibson, *Biblia latina cum Glossa ordinaria: Introduction to the Facsimile Reprint of the Editio Princeps, Adolph Rusch of Strassburg 1480/81* (Turnhout: Brepols, 1992).

[46] Two scriptural citations affect Ranulph's comment here: Apoc. 21.6 and John 4.14.

[47] Gregory the Great, *Epistolae*, Book IX, 52 (PL 77: 991).

[48] Siegfried Wenzel, in a personal conversation with me, identified the source of this proverb as John of Wales' *Ars predicandi*, MS. Bodley 571, fol. 165va.

[49] Plato, *Timaeus*, 27c, in *Plato* (VII), Loeb Classical Library (Cambridge, MA: Harvard University Press, 1952), pp. 48–9. Ranulph depends heavily on Basevorn throughout this chapter; see Charland, *Artes praedicandi* (as in n. 34), pp. 262–4.

[50] Boethius, *The Consolation of Philosophy*, Book III, meter 9 or prose 9; see the Loeb Classical Library edition (Cambridge, MA: Harvard University Press, 1973), pp. 262–75.

[51] Deut. 20.10 recounts this advice. St. Francis of Assisi incorporated the instruction of Luke 9.3, 10.5, and 10.7 to extend "Peace" to everyone into his *Regula non bullata* (ca. 1210), section 14; see the text printed in David Flood and Thaddee Matura, *The Birth of a Movement*, tr. Paul Schwartz and Paul Lachance (Chicago: Franciscan Herald Press, 1975), p. 85.

[52] Augustine, *De doctrina christiana*, IV, 87; see Green (as in n. 9), pp. 234–5.

[53] Paul uses this phrase (or a similar one) to begin his letters to the Romans (1.7), Corinthians (I Cor. 1.3; II Cor. 1.2), Ephesians (1.2), Philippians (1.2), Colossians (1.3), Thessalonians (1.2), and Galatians (1.3), as well as to Timothy, Titus, and Philemon.

[54] Exploring the differences between sermon constructs favored at Oxford and Paris intrigued Robert of Basevorn; Higden probably developed his interest from Basevorn. In his preface, Ranulph counsels putting the invocation of grace first. Here, he seems to favor the integrated and fluent movement from theme to

antetheme to introduction of the theme, which he labels Oxonian. The Parisian method requires a separate development for the intercessory prayer which would be difficult for an ordinary preacher to create. It should be noted that many other differences exist between sermon formats recommended at Oxford and Paris. Basevorn defines and illustrates them at some length; Ranulph makes a few cursory references to these differences but discusses only those that affect the antetheme.

[55] From the chapter entitled "Two wonderful wells, one in Brittany and the other in Sicily," in Gerald of Wales, *The History and Topography of Ireland*, trans. John J. O'Meara (New York: Penguin, 1982), pp. 63–4.

[56] Is. 63.2 and 1.18 provide backdrop from the Hebrew Scriptures for this phrase; John 4.10 and 11 from the Christian Scriptures.

[57] Joel 2.13 makes a similar statement.

[58] Theories of vision were extensively discussed in the Middle Ages. Euclid, al-Kindi and others believed that the rays by which objects are perceived issue, not from the objects, but from the observer's eye. Aristotle, Avicenna, and most of those concerned with medieval optics disagreed, citing Aristotle's definition of sight as a passive power which cannot emit radiation. See David C. Lindberg, *Theories of Vision from al-Kindi to Kepler* (Chicago: Chicago University Press, 1976), pp. 20–1, 47–50, and passim.

[59] Both stories were well known *exempla* in the Middle Ages. An *exemplum*, a short narrative which conveys a moral lesson, is an effective teaching device, especially when it vivifies the lesson(s) of a sermon. The first *exemplum* above is attributed to Jacques de Vitry, in *Jacob's Well*, ed. A. Brandeis, Early English Text Society, O.S. 115 (London: K. Paul, Trench, Trubner and Co., 1900), p. 110; the second, "The Knight unrepentant at death," appears in many sources; see Frederic Tubach, *Index Exemplorum*, F F Communications 204 (Helsinki: Suomalainen Tiedeakatemia, 1969), #2960.

[60] Augustine, in his *De utilitate credendi, De Genesi ad litteram*, and *De doctrina christiana*, described a multi-level exegetical method, although the fourfold structure cited here is a misunderstanding of these texts. Bede, nevertheless, credited the development of the four senses of Scripture to Augustine, and this is how the attribution passed into the Middle Ages; see Henri de Lubac, *Medieval Exegesis*, vol. 1, trans. Mark Sebanc (Grand Rapids, MI: Eerdmans, 1998), pp. 123–7. Except for labeling the literal sense "historical," Ranulph follows the schematic purportedly described about 1260 by Augustine of Dacia: "Littera gesta docet, quid credas allegoria / Moralis quid agas, quo tendas anagogia." The term "allegory" could be a source of confusion because it sometimes encompassed all the spiritual senses; by the fourteenth century, the "allegorical sense" was frequently termed the "typological sense," connoting something quite different from belief. A fine survey of allegory's significations can be found in de Lubac's *Medieval Exegesis*, vol. 2, trans. E. M. Macierowski (Grand Rapids, MI: Eerdmans, 2000), pp. 83–126.

[61] See Lev. 21.13–4.

[62] The term "writings of the saints" permits a broad application, although the usage "bride of Christ" relates specifically to Paul's *Letter to the Ephesians*, 5.22. In fact, the equation of the Church with the "bride of Christ" was already commonplace by the third century; see *Eusebius' Ecclesiastical History*, Book X, chap. 4, trans. C. F. Cruse (Peabody, MA: Hendrickson, 1998), pp. 367–8.

[63] Augustine, *Confessions and Enchiridion*, ed. and trans. Albert C. Outler (Philadelphia: Westminster Press, 1955), Book IV, chap. 12, p. 87.

[64] Seneca, Epistle XLI, sections 1 and 2: "On the God within us"; see *Ad Lucilium epistolae morales*, ed. Reynolds (as in n. 20), p. 108.

[65] Based on Gen. 24.16: "Puella decora nimis virgoque pulcherrima" and II Kings 22.51, III Kings 2.33, and Ps. 17.51, where David and his progeny are alluded to.

[66] Pseudo-Augustine, *Sermo contra Judaeos, Paganos, et Arianos*, PL 42: 1126. The Virgilian reference is to *Eclogue* IV, lines 6–7, a text which medieval authors claimed to be a prophecy by Virgil about the coming of Christ.

[67] A curious reference to one of the rarely efficacious practices of early medieval society, recounted vividly in the Finnsburh episode of *Beowulf*, lines 1068–1159, and foreshadowing Hrothgar's action in lines 2020ff. of the same epic poem; see *Beowulf*, trans. Seamus Heaney (New York: Farrar, Straus, and Giroux, 2000), pp. 71–81 and 139–41.
[68] The numerous significations of both the elephant and the unicorn are described by Beryl Rowland in *Animals with Human Faces* (Knoxville: University of Tennessee Press, 1973), pp. 70–4 and 152–7. Florence McCulloch discusses the allegorical significations of the unicorn in *Medieval Latin and French Bestiaries*, University of North Carolina Studies in the Romance Languages and Literatures 32 (Chapel Hill: University of North Carolina Press, 1960), pp. 179–83.
[69] Ranulph has an expansive definition of "art," here the practical arts, and probably alludes to the story recounted in Matt. 9.12, Mark 2.17, and Luke 5.31.
[70] *Facta et dicta memorabilia liber*, 4.7.2 (as in n. 17), vol. 1, pp. 282–3.
[71] Cicero, *De amicitia*, XIV, 50; see the Loeb Classical Library edition (Cambridge, MA: Harvard University Press, 1964), pp. 160–1. This proverbial statement can also be found in works by Homer, Empedocles, Aristotle, Theophrastus, Plutarch, Callimachus, and Quintillian; it has a biblical parallel in Eccli. 13.20.
[72] Siegfried Wenzel, in a personal conversation with me, identified Higden's statement as a derivation from John of Wales' "sicut dominus sic et familia sua." Petronius' *Satyricon* 58 is its point of origin; see the Loeb Classical Library edition (Cambridge, MA; Harvard University Press, 1969), pp. 122–3.
[72a] See note 43.
[73] Ranulph copies almost verbatim from Basevorn in this paragraph. Charland *Artes praedicandi* (as in n. 34), p. 272 maintains that this section is derived from Chalcidius' translation of Plato's *Timaeus*, 29E.
[74] Textual variants abound for almost every word in the sentence "Therefore … heaven"; this translation represents a meaningful amalgam of all manuscripts. Aristotle's "ensouled heaven" is developed in his *On the Heavens*, 284a–b; see the Loeb Classical Library edition of this text (Canbridge, MA: Harvard University Press, 1945), pp. 134–5.
[75] Ranulph condenses the fuller explanation given by Basevorn; see Charland *Artes praedicandi* (as in n. 34), pp. 272–3. The hierarchy described here was adopted by several medieval authors; it probably is ultimately derived from Pseudo-Dionysius' *Celestial Hierarchy*, translated into Latin by John Scottus Eriugena; see A. H. Armstrong, *The Cambridge History of Later Greek and Early Medieval Philosophy* (Cambridge, Eng.: Cambridge University Press, 1967), pp. 457–72.
[76] Bernard of Clairvaux, *De gradibus humilitatis et superbiae*, in *Opera Bernardi Clairvallensis*, ed. Jean Leclercq and H. M. Rochais (Rome: Editiones Cistercienses, 1963), vol. 2, pp. 35–7.
[77] Ranulph points to an incorrect etymology here: the equation of the "iu" of *iuvenis* ("young man") with the "iu(n)" of *coniunccio* ("union"). Unfortunately, this type of flaw is almost impossible to illustrate in English.
[78] Cicero refutes this idea in *De senectute*, although it remained a standard medieval topos from Horace's *Art of Poetry* onward; see George R. Coffman, "Old Age from Horace to Chaucer," *Speculum* 9 (1934), pp. 249–77. The joyful youth (traceable to Eccli. 11.9) was also a medieval topos.
[79] Ranulph uses etymology, a favorite intellectual exercise of medieval writers, several times in this treatise; for a survey of the development of etymological thinking, see Ernst Robert Curtius, *European Literature and the Latin Middle Ages* (New York: Pantheon Books, 1953), pp. 495–500.
[80] Augustine expressed interest in pervenient grace in many treatises. A section of his *De gratia et libero arbitrio*, written in 425, seems closest to the sentiment expressed here; see PL 44: 892–93.
[81] Possibly a corruption of Deut. 32.10: "He found them in a wilderness, a wasteland of howling desert."
[82] The Latin "in plura" indicates segments of a division in excess of three.
[83] The imperatives in this paragraph have numerous scriptural loci. For "Trust!", see Matt. 9.2 and 22; for "Look around!", see Luke 18.42; for "Listen!", see Is. 37.17 and 48.2; for "Love!", see Prov. 4.6.

[84] In internal division (*divisio intra*), the preacher straightforwardly uses the vocabulary of the theme to create divisions; in external division (*divisio extra*), the preacher eventually arrives at the words of the theme but does not start with them. For example, to divide "Induamur arma lucis," one starts with the realization that sin strips you, weakens you, and blinds you. Thus, you need to clothe yourself ("induamur"), to strengthen yourself ("arma"), and to enlighten yourself ("lucis"). See the edition of the *Ars concionandi*, in *Bonaventurae Opera Omnia*, vol. 9 (Quaracchi: Typographia Collegii S. Bonaventurae, 1901), pp. 9 and 11, which references Boethius' commentary on Cicero's *Topica*, PL 44: 1054 and 1064. In Boethius, internal division and external division are identified as "locus in ipso" and "locus extrinsecus."

[85] The *Distinctiones fratris Nicholai de Gorran de ordine predicatorum secundum ordinem alphabeti* survives in at least thirty-five manuscripts and begins with the word "abeuncium"; see André Wilmart, "Un répertoire d'exégèse composé en Angleterre vers le début du XIIe siècle," in *Mémorial Lagrange* (Paris: J. Galbalda, 1940), pp. 307–46, at pp. 342–3.

[86] Augustine wrote several expositions which express a "contra" to the machinations of the reprobate; see numerous entries in PL 35 and 36.

[87] The story is recounted in Jud. 29.11ff. In light of her father's vow and her impending death, Jepthe's daughter mourned the fact that she was going to die a virgin. Abelard commemorates the tragic events in "Planctus Virginum Israelis super filia Jepthae Galaditae"; see PL 178: 1819ff.

[88] Discussions of triplicate structures, possibly developed in conjunction with Trinitarian doctrine, were popular from Tertullian onward; see PL 2: 915. Explication by threes was beloved by medieval preachers, teachers, and poets; Hildebert of Lavardin demonstrates this schema's use in poetry; see PL 171: 1388ff.

[89] In this section, Higden truncates some but omits most of Basevorn's prolix discussion of a sermon's tenth (correspondence), eleventh (congruence of correspondence), twelfth (circuitous development), and thirteenth (convolution) "ornaments." The *Ars* seems to stress that determined parts should correspond to other determined parts; even with this restriction Ranulph concludes that this structure is not useful for the people. The pyramidal development, not found in Basevorn, does not provoke a negative response.

[90] Higden's brief, but intriguing, discussion of sermon forms caught the attention of Thomas Penketh, a fifteenth-century manualist who repeats and develops these comments; see MS. Oxford University 36, fols. 245–6.

[91] The many forms of division are treated in Boethius, *Liber de divisione*, PL 64: 877–92.

[92] Michael Haren informs me that Higden comments here on a matter of vital concern to the earlier fourteenth century. Bernard of Clairvaux and, in 1331 and 1332, Pope John XXII had declared that the elect were granted contemplation only of the humanity of Christ before the Last Judgment. Hounded by theologians, John recanted on his deathbed; in 1336, his successor's Constitution, "Benedictus Deus," made direct entry into heaven a church dogma. Prior to this resolution, Ranulph's fellow manualist, Thomas Waleys, became embroiled in this controversy and was imprisoned as a result; see Dorothy Grosser, *Thomas Waleys: On the Manner of Composing Sermons*, unpublished M.A. thesis (Cornell University, 1949), pp. iii–v.

[93] The four exegetical levels, as Ranulph defines them here, are not identical with those listed at n. 60 and n. 103. Variations were commonplace, however; see de Lubac's whole commentary on "Opposing Lists" in *Medieval Exegesis*, vol. 1 (as in n. 60), pp. 83–116, especially pp. 112–15.

[94] A development of I John 1.7: "And the blood of Jesus Christ … cleanses us from all sin."

[95] The words "vocis significatio" bring to mind the virulent debate about universals which broke the medieval scholarly world into realist and nominalist camps. Whether Ranulph is relating directly to this circumstance or not, he clearly maintains that university exercises have no place in the development of effective preaching. Note that the Latin word for "studying" is "reading," a usage common in Britain even today.

[96] These words of Wis. 10.10, with the addition of "Dominus," constitute the common responsory of the Divine Office for bishops, confessors, and doctors of the Church.
[97] The scope and ramifications of these terms are discussed at length in Boethius' *Liber de diffinitione*, PL 64: 891–910.
[98] Porphyry, *Liber praedicabilium*, chap. 3, "de specie"; see Porphyry, *On Aristotle's Categories*, trans. Steven K. Strange (Ithaca: Cornell, 1992), p. 73.
[99] By using *funiculis* ("cords"), Ranulph may have thought he was correcting Basevorn, whose *funibus* ("meshes") is a quote from Prov. 5.22. Some conflation with forms of the word *funiculus* in Eccl. 4.12 and Is. 5.18 may also have occurred.
[100] David and Nathan address each other in quasi-enthymemes in II Kings 7 and I Par. 17. Matt. 21.33–44 makes reference to the owner of a vineyard who might qualify as an "agricola" or farmer; Mark 12.2–9 and Luke 20.9–15 recount the same story.
[101] The idea of extra-penitential "satisfaction" was unknown to patristic tradition. Anselm's *Cur Deus Homo* (I, 20–21) pointed to the necessity for Christ's taking on responsibility for this satisfaction; Thomas Aquinas softened Anselm's "necessity" by investigating the many ways in which satisfaction occurred (see *Summa theologiae*, suppl., q. 12–15). Pope Clement VI's bull, "Unigenitus Dei Filius" (1343), may have prompted further questioning about the concept of satisfaction.
[102] Chapter V discusses the caution with which preachers must approach their office.
[103] Osee 14.6 says that "Israel grows like a lily." "The just man grows like a palm tree," according to Ps. 91.13.
[104] The literal sense — or what the text says — has becomes the "historical" or "narrative of deeds" in this section, and in the first example "allegory" functions typologically. However, the word and concept, "literal," is reinstated in the following remarks about "Jerusalem," and allegory reverts to Augustine of Dacia's "quid credas."
[105] What and who constitute the Church is a perennial theological question which was answered variably in the medieval centuries. The statement made here, however, seems an expansion of Augustine's view (supported by Gregory the Great) according to which the Church comprises in a solidarity of Christian faith all the saints of both covenants; see PL 35: 1722–3 and PL 37: 1159, as well as F. X. Lawlor, "Mystical Body of Christ," in *New Catholic Encyclopedia* (New York: McGraw-Hill, 1967), vol. X, pp. 166–70, at pp. 168–9.
[106] Ranulph could be referring to the commonplace decoration of English rood screens where Mary and John are placed on either side of the crucified Christ. This may have been the situation at St. Werburgh's Abbey in Chester, although such cannot be currently verified as the present rood screen is the nineteenth-century creation of Sir Gilbert Scott. See Charles Hiatt, *The Cathedral Church of Chester* (London: George Bell & Sons, 1897), p. 48.
[107] Boethius, *The Consolation of Philosophy*, Book III, prose 3 and meter 7 (as in n. 50), pp. 256–9.
[108] The feminine pronoun is dictated by the preaching context, although the scriptural verse has a definitively masculine reference.
[109] The equation of "Jacob" with "Supplantor" derives from Gen. 27.36: "Then he said, 'Must he, true to his name Jacob, supplant me now a second time? He took my birthright and now he has taken my blessing.'"
[110] The triple enemy — the world, the flesh, and the devil — was not commonly cited in theological and monastic writings before 1000; championed by several prestigious churchmen, however, it became a topos current from the twelfth century onward; see Siegfried Wenzel, "The Three Enemies of Man," *Mediaeval Studies* 29 (1967), pp. 47–66.
[111] See above. The "triplex" emphasis is not obvious in chapter VII; it is noteworthy here.
[112] Ex. 12.27 reads "transitus Domini est"; Lev. 23.5 reads "phase (pascha) Domini est."

[113] Ranulph may be referring to the doctrine of transubstantiation. *Transsubstantiatio* seems to have been first used by Roland Bandinelli in the mid-twelfth century. Medieval controversies about the word's meaning hinged on whether or not the whole essence of the Eucharistic bread and wine was changed. Alexander of Hales' view prevailed in the fourteenth century: "an actual being, without being destroyed or annihilated, is changed according to its whole substance into another actual being." See *Sacramentum Mundi*, ed. Karl Rahner (New York: Heder and Herder, 1970), vol. 6, pp. 292–5.

[114] Augustine studied the relationship between reason and authority in many texts, but most clearly in *De vera religione*, chap. 24–28; see PL 34: 141ff.

[115] Basevorn mentions coloration in Chapter 14, but picks up on its usages (even extending his illustration of similar endings to four-word phrases) almost as an afterthought at the end of his *Forma praedicandi*. Ranulph stops at three, satisfied at having shown how these patterns are established. The passage defies felicitous English translation; consequently, the Latin words have been appended with their similar endings italicized.

[116] *Versus*, ordinarily "verse" or "line," probably means "sentence" when related to a prose text like a sermon. Ranulph coordinates punctuation with certain rhythmical patterns found in Latin word groups. Terms like *punctus flexus* ("comma") and *punctus medius* ("semicolon") were commonplace in the system of liturgical "positurae," a feature of monastic culture showing where were the appropriate pauses in chanting and reading; see M. B. Parkes, *Pause and Effect: An Introduction to the History of Punctuation in the West* (Berkeley: University of California Press, 1993), pp. 35–8, 306, 303–04, 307.

[117] Mark Riley suggests that the cadences specified here can be translated into English thus: for *francis origine*, "Frankish in origin"; for *genere francus*, "by origin Frankish"; for *schemate generoso*, "lovely in Athabasca."

[118] This is the *Ars*' only reference to the word "distinction," a term originally signifying the exploration of a word's theoretical relationships. The distinction's widespread acceptance in the later twelfth century is linked to the emergence of the thematic sermon by Richard Rouse and Mary Rouse in "*Statim invenire*: Schools, Preachers and New Attitudes to the Page," in *Renaissance and Renewal in the Twelfth Century*, ed. Robert Benson and Giles Constable (Cambridge, MA: Harvard University Press, 1982), pp. 201–25, at pp. 213–18. By the fourteenth century, *distinctio* was often related conceptually to the subdivision; see MS Balliol 179, fol. 324r. Here, Ranulph seems to be echoing Basevorn's usage, which defines *distinctio* as a section of text.

[119] Chapter I begins with "Ad"; Chapter II with "Rectitudo"; Chapter III with "Sanctitudo," and so forth.

Index of Proper Names (excluding biblical personages)

Ancient and Medieval Authors

Selected Modern Authors

(not including items listed in the Bibliography on pp. 24–7)

Subject Index